100

classic and contemporary meals, family favourites and impressive recipes you can absolutely rely on

maincourses
for every occasion

Recipes for poultry and meat, fish and shellfish, salads, vegetarian options and one-pot meals, in 400 photographs

CONSULTANT EDITOR: JENNI FLEETWOOD

southwater

This edition is published by Southwater, an imprint of Anness
Publishing Ltd, Hermes House,
88–89 Blackfriars Road, London SE1 8HA;
tel. 020 7401 2077; fax 020 7633 9499

www.southwaterbooks.com; www.annesspublishing.com

If you like the images in this book and would like to
investigate using them for publishing, promotions or
advertising, please visit our website www.practicalpictures.com
for more information.

UK agent: The Manning Partnership Ltd;
tel. 01225 478444; fax 01225 478440;
sales@manning-partnership.co.uk
UK distributor: Grantham Book Services Ltd;
tel. 01476 541080; fax 01476 541061;
orders@gbs.tbs-ltd.co.uk
North American agent/distributor: National Book Network; tel.
301 459 3366; fax 301 429 5746; www.nbnbooks.com
Australian agent/distributor: Pan Macmillan Australia; tel.
1300 135 113; fax 1300 135 103;
customer.service@macmillan.com.au
New Zealand agent/distributor: David Bateman Ltd;
tel. (09) 415 7664; fax (09) 415 8892

Publisher: Joanna Lorenz
Senior Managing Editor: Conor Kilgallon
Editors: Joy Wotton amd Elizabeth Woodland
Production Controller: Lee Sargent
Cover Designer: Terry Jeavons
Designers: Nigel Partridge, Steers McGillan Ltd
and Sarah Williams
Recipes: Alex Barker, Carla Capalbo, Lesley Chamberlain,
Jacqueline Clark, Roz Denny, Patrizia Diemling, Matthew
Drennan, Joanna Farrow, Valerie Ferguson, Jenni Fleetwood,
Silvano Franco, Yasuko Fukuoka, Shirley Gill, Brian Glover,
Nicola Graimes, Juliet Harbutt, Deh-Ta Hsiung, Christine
Ingram, Manisha Kanani, Emi Kasuko, Lucy Knox, Gilly Love,
Lesley Mackley, Norma MacMillan, Jane Milton, Sallie Morris,
Anne Sheasby, Marlena Spieler, Linda Tubby, Laura
Washburn, Kate Whiteman
Photographers: Nicki Dowey, Michelle Garrett, Amanda
Heywood, Janine Hosegood, David Jordan, Dave King, William
Lingwood, Thomas Odulate, Craig Robertson and Sam Stowell

ETHICAL TRADING POLICY

Because of our ongoing ecological investment programme,
you, as our customer, can have the pleasure and reassurance
of knowing that a tree is being cultivated on your behalf to
naturally replace the materials used to make the book you are
holding. For further information about this scheme, go to
www.annesspublishing.com/trees

Previously published as part of a larger volume,
Classic Main Courses

NOTES

Bracketed terms are intended for American readers.
For all recipes, quantities are given in both metric and imperial
measures and, where appropriate, in standard cups and spoons.
Follow one set of measures, but not a mixture, because they
are not interchangeable.
Standard spoon and cup measures are level. 1 tsp = 5ml,
1 tbsp = 15ml, 1 cup = 250ml/8fl oz.
Australian standard tablespoons are 20ml. Australian
readers should use 3 tsp in place of 1 tbsp for measuring
small quantities.
American pints are 16fl oz/2 cups. American readers
should use 20fl oz/2.5 cups in place of 1 pint when
measuring liquids.
Electric oven temperatures in this book are for conventional
ovens. When using a fan oven, the temperature will probably
need to be reduced by about 10–20°C/20–40°F. Since ovens
vary, you should check with your manufacturer's instruction
book for guidance.
The nutritional analysis given for each recipe is calculated per
portion (i.e. serving or item), unless otherwise stated. If the recipe
gives a range, such as Serves 4–6, then the nutritional analysis
will be for the smaller portion size, i.e. 6 servings. Measurements
for sodium do not include salt added to taste.
Medium (US large) eggs are used unless otherwise stated.

Main front cover image shows Pasta with Tomatoes and
Shellfish – for recipe, see page 45

CONTENTS

INTRODUCTION

Main dishes are the most important part of any meal, and often the course around which all others revolve – they are the pivotal part of every meal.

However, the main course still has something of an image problem. Appetizers and desserts are seen as new and exciting, but main courses seem to have earned adjectives like "comforting", "robust", "satisfying" and "rib-sticking". When it comes to planning a special occasion meal, most of us have no difficulty in deciding what to serve for the first and final courses – it's what comes between the first and the last that proves to be the most problematic.

Look no further. With this compilation of 100 classic recipes you will never be stuck for inspiration again. In fact, the difficulty will lie in deciding what to choose, whether it be a colourful healthy salad, a pasta dish or the full works in the form of a meat or chicken roast or a hearty casserole.

THE TRADITIONAL MAIN COURSE

The days of the marathon meal have long gone – it is very unlikely when dining with family and friends that you'll be presented with an appetizer or soup leading to the fish course, followed by the meat course, a sorbet (sherbet), the dessert, and then the cheese and, finally, coffee. Today it is perfectly acceptable simply to serve guests a satisfying pasta dish or casserole with lots of deliciously crusty bread for mopping up the juices or a home-baked pie with a refreshing side salad. Now you can dispense with soups and appetizers altogether, layout a table snacks, or you can simply offer guests canapés with their drinks as they arrive.

The classic meat-and-two-veg theme has also vanished as more people have either become vegetarians or simply chosen to limit the amount of meat they eat. Today, a main course can be a roulade, a pie, a risotto, a substantial soup – or anything else you

choose to serve. A curry with a cooling raita and plump Peshwari naan would go down well, as would a home-made pizza with a stylish topping. It is even perfectly acceptable to serve sausages and mash and, if you present the sausages on a mound of spicy mashed sweet potato and surround them with caramelized onions – you'll be recreating a fashionable restaurant dish that will delight and please your guests.

Vegetables can star in an appetizer or salad as a separate course. When serving vegetables, consider a fresh medley of steamed cubed carrots, leeks and potato, for instance, or simply a roast mixture of your favourite vegetables. That way you cut down on last-minute cooking, and avoid being in the kitchen for too long when your guests have just arrived.

Whatever you choose to serve, the meal should always be balanced in terms of flavours, colours and textures. For example, it wouldn't be a good idea to serve a creamy mousse as a main course then follow it with a silky-smooth dessert, or to serve a juicy Thai stew or curry after a soup. If the main course is quite dry, for example a country meat loaf, it should be accompanied by a succulent side dish, such as creamed leeks or mushrooms. It also makes good sense to try and avoid using the same ingredients in successive courses as repeatedly encountering the same flavours and textures can be boring.

GARNISH YOUR FOOD

The appearance of the food on the plate has become just as important as the actual dish itself, so do give some thought to the colours and shapes of the ingredients used in the dish. Just make sure the garnish is appropriate to the dish you are serving – lemon wedges are perfect with a fish dish, a fresh sprig of herbs pair well with a vegetable stew, and spring onions finish off any curry.

Left: Elegant and well-presented food creates a pretty and sophisticated look to the dinner.

Above: Steaming is a classic Chinese way of cooking fish. It is a very healthy method of cooking and simple to do.

STRESS-FREE COOKING

When planning any meal, make life easy for yourself by preparing or cooking as much as possible ahead of time. Ease a heavy workload by using kitchen appliances such as the microwave oven and food processor. Make use of your fridge and freezer – many dishes are even better when made ahead of time as this allows the flavours to infuse.

Cooking and sharing good food with friends and family is one of life's greatest pleasures, and with this book, you are sure to find the perfect recipe to impress all your guests.

Left: A filling risotto flavoured with four different cheeses is a substantial and delicious alternative for a vegetarian friend or family member.

PREPARING AND COOKING AHEAD

The marvellous thing about many main dishes is that they can be prepared in advance and cooked when required. Not only does this keep stress levels low but it also ensures that success levels remain high. Slow-cooked dishes, such as casseroles and stews, are also a boon as they need little attention and reward the cook by quietly gaining in flavour as they simmer in the oven. At the other end of the spectrum are dishes such as stir-fries and salads, which need little or no cooking. This time, careful preparation is the key. Salad leaves can be washed and dried, then bagged and put in the refrigerator. Not only will they be ready to toss together at the last minute, but they will also become crisper on standing. Stir-fry vegetables should all be cut to a similar size. Although it is not a good idea to do this too far ahead, because valuable nutrients will be lost, such advance preparation is helpful when you know you will be in a hurry later.

COOKING IN ADVANCE

Dishes such as stews, curries and casseroles often benefit from being made the day before they are to be served. This allows time for the flavours of the different ingredients to meld. If it is more convenient, you can cook dishes like this even further ahead,

Right: The components of a salad can be prepared in advance, ready for last-minute assembly when required.

freeze them and defrost them when you need to. The food must be cold before being placed in the freezer. Let it cool for a little, then place the dish or pot in a sink of very cold or iced water to accelerate the chilling process. Some china is designed to withstand extremes of temperature and can be used in both the oven and the freezer, but it is not recommended that you switch between the two without either allowing the hot food to cool, or the frozen food to thaw completely. It is best to thaw dishes overnight in the refrigerator. If you use a microwave for thawing, always follow the instructions in your handbook, and stir the stew or casserole frequently as it thaws, to make sure the item thaws evenly. When thawing a large block of frozen food in the microwave, it is a good idea to defrost it in short bursts, with a resting time between each, so that the heat that is generated spreads throughout the defrosting food and is not concentrated only in certain areas.

Rather than tie up a favourite straight-sided casserole or gratin dish by transferring it to the freezer for several weeks, tip the contents into a pan or dish, then wash the casserole or

dish and line it with microwave-proof film (wrap). Return the casserole or stew to the dish, and place it in the freezer. Lift out the contents when frozen, then double wrap and label the block and return it to the freezer. When you want to serve the food, just unwrap the block and return it to the original dish for thawing and reheating.

LEFTOVERS

As with freshly cooked food intended for the freezer, leftovers should be cooled quickly if they are to be kept for another meal. Leaving leftovers in their original dishes to cool slowly in a warm kitchen could encourage harmful bacteria to multiply in the food, causing illness. So transfer leftovers to clean, cold dishes and as soon as they have cooled, cover them and place them in the refrigerator. Use the next day and reheat thoroughly.

Leftovers can also be recycled, and the remains of dishes such as chicken, game or meat casseroles, can be used as a filling for a pie. A simple fish pie, topped with mashed potato, can easily be transformed into hot, crisp fish cakes. However, you should not rework ingredients more than once.

Left: Cooking casseroles and stews a day ahead is not only convenient, but also improves the flavour of the dish.

FREEZING TIPS AND TECHNIQUES

• Cool food rapidly, then wrap securely and label – with a description, the date and number of servings. If you are freezing several items at the same time, use the fast-freeze facility on your freezer.

• Hearty soups and stews freeze well, unless they contain chopped potatoes, rice, barley or pasta, which lose texture and become mushy on freezing. If these ingredients are included in the recipe, add them after thawing, then simmer the soup or stew until these ingredients are fully cooked.

• Stews and casseroles freeze well, but leave a little head room in the container to allow the liquid to expand during the freezing process.

• Blot the surface of a stew to remove surplus fat before freezing or chill so that fat solidifies and can be lifted off. Fat can become rancid, especially if a dish is frozen for a long time. Omit bacon unless you are freezing a composite dish for just a few weeks.

• Make sure that any pieces of meat or poultry in a dish that includes a sauce or gravy are fully submerged in the liquid, to reduce the risk of their drying out in the freezer.

• Although fish in sauce can be frozen, the thawed and reheated dish will not taste so good as when it was originally made, so it is better to cook such dishes on the day you serve them.

• Small items, such as meatballs, burgers and fish cakes, freeze well. Open-freeze them on trays, then wrap individually so that you can remove just as many as you need at any time.

Rice advice

Although rice can be cooked ahead of time and frozen or chilled for reheating, it is essential that it is cooled quickly and thoroughly before being stored. It should be reheated until it is very hot and served immediately. Never keep cooked rice warm for long periods. These precautions are necessary to avoid food poisoning.

STORAGE TIMES

• Meat casseroles and stews improve in taste if they are cooked ahead, but they should not be kept in the refrigerator for more than 2 days before being reheated and served.

• Soups can be frozen for a period of up to 3 months. Leave adequate space when wrapping the container to allow for expansion on freezing.

• Casseroles or stews containing bacon, pork or ham should not be frozen for more than 6 weeks. If these ingredients are not present, optimum freezing time is 2 months.

• Minced (ground) beef dishes, such as chilli con carne, freeze well. These can be stored for up to 2 months.

• Curries freeze well for up to 3 months, but the flavour of the spices deteriorates after this.

• Cooked pasta dishes, such as lasagne and cannelloni, can be frozen for up to 3 months.

• Cooked fish dishes in sauce can be frozen for up to 1 month only. Frozen fish cakes should be used within 2 months.

Above: Make the most of your freezer by batch-cooking suitable dishes, such as stews, curries, lasagnes, and casseroles.

REHEATING

It is important always to make sure that a dish has thawed completely before reheating. Food should be piping hot all the way through before being served, especially if it contains meat on the bone. Timing will depend on the specific ingredients and the quantities being used, but as a guide, a chicken casserole that has been thawed to room temperature should be reheated for 45–60 minutes in an oven preheated to 200°C/400°F/Gas 6. Stir the casserole and check its temperature occasionally. Such delicate foods as fish should not be reheated for so long that their flavour and texture is spoiled. If you reheat foods in a pan on top of the stove, stir them frequently to prevent them from sticking to the base of the pan. If you use the microwave to reheat food, then follow the instructions in your handbook for the precise cooking time.

SOUPS, SALADS & LIGHT MEALS

Whether you're cooking for the family, or having friends

around for a casual supper, nothing beats a bowl of steaming

soup on a cold day. Soup spells comfort as well as flavour, and

when the soup is a substantial one, such as Pot Cooked Udon

in Miso or Chicken and Leek Soup with Prunes, there's no need

for elaborate accompaniments. For a light summer lunch, Prawn

Salad would be the perfect choice, or, as the weather cools, you

might like to introduce a hint of warmth with a Warm Salad

with Ham, Egg and Asparagus.

Spinach and Rice Soup

Use very young spinach leaves to prepare this light and fresh-tasting soup.

<u>SERVES FOUR</u>

INGREDIENTS

675g/1½lb fresh spinach
  leaves, washed
45ml/3 tbsp extra virgin olive oil
1 small onion, finely chopped
2 garlic cloves, finely chopped
1 small fresh red chilli, seeded
  and finely chopped
225g/8oz/generous 1 cup
  risotto rice
1.2 litres/2 pints/5 cups
  vegetable stock
salt and ground black pepper
shavings of pared Parmesan or
  Pecorino cheese, to serve

1 Place the spinach in a large pan with just the water that clings to its leaves after washing. Add a large pinch of salt. Heat gently until the spinach has wilted, then remove from the heat and drain, reserving any liquid.

2 Either chop the spinach finely using a large kitchen knife or place in a food processor and process the leaves to a fairly coarse purée.

3 Heat the oil in a large pan. Add the onion, garlic and chilli and cook gently for 4–5 minutes, until softened. Stir in the rice until well coated, then pour in the stock and reserved spinach liquid. Bring to the boil, lower the heat and simmer for 10 minutes.

4 Add the spinach and season with salt and pepper to taste. Cook the soup for a further 5–7 minutes, until the rice is tender. Taste and adjust the seasoning, if necessary. Ladle into heated bowls, top with the shavings of Parmesan or Pecorino and serve immediately.

COOK'S TIP
Buy Parmesan or Pecorino cheese in the piece from a reputable supplier, and it will be full of flavour and easy to grate or shave with a vegetable peeler.

VARIATION
Substitute Swiss chard for the spinach.

Per portion: Energy 340Kcal/1431kJ; Protein 9.2g; Carbohydrate 52.3g, of which sugars 3.4g; Fat 11.9g, of which saturates 1.9g; Cholesterol 0mg; Calcium 320mg; Fibre 4g; Sodium 449mg.

LOBSTER BISQUE

BISQUE IS A LUXURIOUS, VELVETY SOUP, WHICH CAN BE MADE WITH ANY CRUSTACEANS.

SERVES SIX

INGREDIENTS

- 500g/1¼lb fresh lobster
- 75g/3oz/6 tbsp butter
- 1 onion, chopped
- 1 carrot, diced
- 1 celery stick, diced
- 45ml/3 tbsp brandy, plus extra for serving (optional)
- 250ml/8fl oz/1 cup dry white wine
- 1 litre/1¾ pints/4 cups fish stock
- 15ml/1 tbsp tomato purée (paste)
- 75g/3oz/scant ½ cup long grain rice
- 1 fresh bouquet garni
- 150ml/¼ pint/⅔ cup double (heavy) cream, plus extra to garnish
- salt, ground white pepper and cayenne pepper

1 Cut the lobster into pieces. Melt half the butter in a large pan, add the vegetables and cook over a low heat until soft. Put in the lobster and stir until the shell on each piece turns red.

2 Pour over the brandy and set it alight. When the flames die down, add the wine and boil until reduced by half. Pour in the fish stock and simmer for 2–3 minutes. Remove the lobster.

3 Stir in the tomato purée and rice, add the bouquet garni and cook until the rice is tender. Meanwhile, remove the lobster meat from the shell and return the shells to the pan. Dice the lobster meat and set it aside.

COOK'S TIP
It is best to buy a live lobster, chilling it in the freezer until it is comatose and then killing it just before cooking. If you can't face the procedure, use a cooked lobster; take care not to over-cook the flesh. Stir for only 30–60 seconds.

4 When the rice is cooked, discard all the larger pieces of shell. Tip the mixture into a blender or food processor and process to a purée. Press the purée through a fine sieve placed over the clean pan. Stir the mixture, then heat until almost boiling. Season with salt, pepper and cayenne, then lower the heat and stir in the cream. Dice the remaining butter and whisk it into the bisque. Add the diced lobster meat and serve immediately. If you like, pour a small spoonful of brandy into each soup bowl and swirl in a little extra cream.

Per portion: Energy 406Kcal/1684kJ; Protein 20.3g; Carbohydrate 13.7g, of which sugars 3.1g; Fat 25.2g, of which saturates 15g; Cholesterol 153mg; Calcium 84mg; Fibre 0.7g; Sodium 365mg.

PUMPKIN, RICE AND CHICKEN SOUP

THIS IS A WARM, COMFORTING CHICKEN SOUP WHOSE SPICE AND ORANGE RIND GARNISH WILL BRIGHTEN THE DULLEST WINTER DAY. FOR AN EVEN MORE SUBSTANTIAL MEAL, ADD A LITTLE RICE.

SERVES FOUR

INGREDIENTS
   1 wedge of pumpkin, about 450g/1lb
   15ml/1 tbsp sunflower oil
   25g/1oz/2 tbsp butter
   6 green cardamom pods
   2 leeks, chopped
   115g/4oz/generous ½ cup basmati
    rice, soaked
   350ml/12fl oz/1½ cups milk
   salt and ground black pepper
   generous strips of pared orange rind,
    to garnish
For the chicken stock
   2 chicken quarters
   1 onion, quartered
   2 carrots, chopped
   1 celery stalk, chopped
   6–8 peppercorns
   900ml/1½ pints/3¾ cups water

1 First make the chicken stock. Place the chicken quarters, onion, carrots, celery and peppercorns in a large, heavy pan. Pour in the water and bring to the boil over a low heat. Skim off any scum on the surface if necessary, then lower the heat, cover and simmer gently for 1 hour.

2 Strain the chicken stock into a clean, large bowl, discarding the vegetables. Skin and bone one or both chicken pieces and cut the flesh into strips. (If not using both chicken pieces for the soup, reserve the other piece for another recipe.)

3 Peel the pumpkin and remove all the seeds and pith, so that you have about 350g/12oz flesh. Cut the flesh into 2.5cm/1in cubes.

4 Heat the oil and butter in a pan, add the cardamom pods and cook for about 2–3 minutes, until slightly swollen. Add the leeks and pumpkin. Cook, stirring, for 3–4 minutes over a medium heat, then lower the heat, cover and sweat for 5 minutes more, or until the pumpkin is quite soft, stirring once or twice.

5 Measure out 600ml/1 pint/2½ cups of the stock and add to the pumpkin mixture. Bring to the boil, then lower the heat, cover and simmer gently for 10–15 minutes, until the pumpkin is soft.

6 Pour the remaining stock into a measuring jug (cup) and make up with water to 300ml/½ pint/1¼ cups. Drain the rice and put it into a pan. Pour in the stock, bring to the boil, then simmer for about 10 minutes, until the rice is tender. Add seasoning to taste.

7 Remove and discard the cardamom pods, then process the soup in a blender or food processor until smooth. Pour it back into a clean saucepan and stir in the milk, chicken and rice (with any stock that has not been absorbed). Heat until simmering.

8 Ladle into warm bowls, garnish with the strips of pared orange rind and freshly ground black pepper and serve immediately with wholemeal (wholewheat) bread.

Per portion: Energy 336Kcal/1406kJ; Protein 25.4g; Carbohydrate 33.9g, of which sugars 7.8g; Fat 11g, of which saturates 5g; Cholesterol 71mg; Calcium 168mg; Fibre 2.9g; Sodium 122mg.

CHICKEN AND LEEK SOUP WITH PRUNES

THIS RECIPE IS BASED ON THE TRADITIONAL SCOTTISH SOUP, COCK-A-LEEKIE. THE UNUSUAL COMBINATION OF LEEKS AND PRUNES IS SURPRISINGLY DELICIOUS.

SERVES SIX

INGREDIENTS
  1 chicken, weighing about 2kg/4¼lb
  900g/2lb leeks
  1 fresh bay leaf
  a few each fresh parsley stalks
    and thyme sprigs
  1 large carrot, thickly sliced
  2.4 litres/4 pints/10 cups
    chicken or beef stock
  115g/4oz/generous ½ cup
    pearl barley
  400g/14oz ready-to-eat prunes
  salt and ground black pepper
  chopped fresh parsley,
    to garnish

1 Cut the breast portions off the chicken and set aside. Place the remaining carcass in a large pan. Cut half the leeks into 5cm/2in lengths and add them to the pan. Tie the bay leaf, parsley and thyme into a bouquet garni and add to the pan with the carrot and the stock. Bring to the boil, then reduce the heat and cover. Simmer gently for 1 hour. Skim off any scum when the water first boils and during simmering.

2 Add the chicken breast portions and cook for another 30 minutes, until they are just cooked. Leave until cool enough to handle, then strain the stock into a bowl. Reserve all the chicken meat. Discard all the skin, bones, cooked vegetables and herbs. Skim as much fat as you can from the stock, then return it to the pan.

3 Meanwhile, rinse the pearl barley thoroughly in a sieve under cold running water, then cook it in a large pan of boiling water over a medium heat for about 10 minutes. Drain, rinse well again and drain thoroughly.

4 Add the pearl barley to the stock. Bring to the boil over a medium heat, then lower the heat and cook very gently for 15–20 minutes, until the barley is just cooked and tender. Season the soup with 5ml/1 tsp salt and black pepper to taste.

5 Add the prunes. Slice the remaining leeks and add them to the pan. Bring to the boil, then simmer for 10 minutes, or until the leeks are just cooked.

6 Slice the chicken breast portions and add them to the soup with the remaining chicken meat, sliced or cut into neat pieces. Reheat if necessary, then ladle the soup into deep plates and sprinkle with chopped parsley.

Per portion: Energy 606Kcal/2533kJ; Protein 44.9g; Carbohydrate 40g, of which sugars 23.9g; Fat 30.8g, of which saturates 8.4g; Cholesterol 220mg; Calcium 45mg; Fibre 4.2g; Sodium 405mg.

POT-COOKED UDON IN MISO SOUP

UDON IS A WHITE WHEAT NOODLE, MORE POPULAR IN THE SOUTH AND WEST OF JAPAN THAN THE NORTH. IT IS EATEN WITH VARIOUS HOT AND COLD SAUCES AND SOUPS. HERE, IN THIS DISH KNOWN AS MISO NIKOMI UDON, THE NOODLES ARE COOKED IN A CLAY POT WITH A RICH MISO SOUP.

SERVES FOUR

INGREDIENTS
200g/7oz skinless, chicken breast
   fillets
10ml/2 tsp sake
2 abura-age (thin deep fried tofu)
900ml/1½ pints/3¾ cups dashi
   stock, or the same amount of water
   and 7.5ml/1½ tsp dashi-no-moto
6 large fresh shiitake mushrooms,
   stalks removed, quartered
4 spring onions (scallions), trimmed
   and chopped into 3mm/⅛in lengths
30ml/2 tbsp mirin
about 90g/3½oz aka miso or
   hatcho miso
300g/11oz dried udon noodles
4 eggs
seven spice powder (optional)

1 Cut the chicken into bitesize pieces and place in a shallow dish. Sprinkle with sake and leave to marinate in a cool place for 15 minutes.

2 Put the abura-age in a sieve and thoroughly rinse with hot water from the kettle to wash off the oil.

3 Drain on kitchen paper and cut each abura-age into four squares.

4 To make the soup, heat the dashi stock in a large pan. When it has come to the boil, add the chicken pieces, shiitake mushrooms and abura-age and cook for 5 minutes over a medium heat. Remove the pan from the heat and add the spring onions.

5 Put the mirin and miso paste into a small bowl. Scoop 30ml/2 tbsp soup from the pan and mix this in well.

6 To cook the udon, boil at least 2 litres/ 3½ pints/9 cups water in a large pan. The water should not come higher than two-thirds the depth of the pan. Cook the udon for 6 minutes and drain.

7 Put the udon in one large flameproof clay pot or casserole (or divide among four small pots). Mix the miso paste into the soup and check the taste. Add more miso if required.

8 Ladle in enough soup to cover the udon, and arrange the soup ingredients on top of the udon.

9 Put the soup on a medium heat and break the eggs on top. When the soup bubbles, wait for 1 minute, then cover and remove from the heat. Leave to stand for 2 minutes. Serve with seven spice powder, if you like.

Per portion: Energy 666Kcal/2781kJ; Protein 49.6g; Carbohydrate 61.9g, of which sugars 1.8g; Fat 24.4g, of which saturates 1.8g; Cholesterol 225mg; Calcium 1536mg; Fibre 0.7g; Sodium 655mg.

HOT AND SOUR SOUP

ONE OF CHINA'S MOST POPULAR SOUPS, THIS IS FAMED FOR ITS CLEVER BALANCE OF FLAVOURS. THE "HOT" COMES FROM PEPPER; THE "SOUR" FROM VINEGAR. SIMILAR SOUPS ARE FOUND THROUGHOUT ASIA, SOME RELYING ON CHILLIES AND LIME JUICE TO PROVIDE THE ESSENTIAL FLAVOUR CONTRAST.

SERVES SIX

INGREDIENTS

4–6 dried shiitake mushrooms
2–3 small pieces of wood ear (dried
  Chinese mushroom) and a few
  golden needles (lily buds) (optional)
115g/4oz pork fillet (tenderloin), cut
  into fine strips
45ml/3 tbsp cornflour (cornstarch)
150ml/^{1}/4 pint/^{2}/3 cup water
15–30ml/1–2 tbsp sunflower oil
1 small onion, finely chopped
1.5 litres/2^1/2 pints/6^1/4 cups beef or
  chicken stock, or 2 × 300g/11oz
  cans consommé made up to the full
  quantity with water
150g/5oz drained fresh firm
  tofu, diced
60ml/4 tbsp rice vinegar
15ml/1 tbsp light soy sauce
1 egg, beaten
5 ml/1 tsp sesame oil
salt and ground white or black pepper
2–3 spring onions (scallions),
  shredded, to garnish

1 Place the shiitake mushrooms in a bowl, with the pieces of wood ear and the golden needles, if using. Add sufficient warm water to cover and leave to soak for about 30 minutes. Drain the mushrooms, reserving the soaking water. Cut off and discard the mushroom stems and slice the caps finely. Trim away any tough stem from the wood ears, then chop them finely. Using kitchen string, tie the golden needles into a bundle.

2 Lightly dust the strips of pork fillet with some of the cornflour. Mix the remaining cornflour to a smooth paste with the measured water.

3 Heat the oil in a wok or pan and cook the onion until soft. Increase the heat and cook the pork until it changes colour. Add the stock or consommé, mushrooms, soaking water, and wood ears and golden needles, if using. Bring to the boil, then simmer for 15 minutes.

4 Discard the golden needles, lower the heat and stir in the cornflour paste to thicken. Add the tofu, vinegar, soy sauce, and salt and pepper.

5 Bring the soup to just below boiling point, then drizzle in the beaten egg by letting it drop from a whisk (or to be authentic, the fingertips) so that it forms threads in the soup. Stir in the sesame oil and serve at once, garnished with spring onion shreds.

Per portion: Energy 169Kcal/709kJ; Protein 7.6g; Carbohydrate 19.7g, of which sugars 0.8g; Fat 7.2g, of which saturates 1.2g; Cholesterol 44mg; Calcium 141mg; Fibre 0.2g; Sodium 351mg.

CAESAR SALAD

THIS MUCH-ENJOYED SALAD WAS CREATED BY CAESAR CARDINI IN TIJUANA IN 1924. BE SURE TO USE CRISP LETTUCE AND ADD THE SOFT EGGS AND GARLIC CROÛTONS AT THE LAST MINUTE.

3 Add the remaining olive oil to the salad leaves and season with salt and pepper. Toss to coat well.

4 Break the soft-boiled eggs on top. Sprinkle with the lemon juice and toss to combine the ingredients.

5 Add the grated Parmesan cheese and anchovies, if using, then toss again.

SERVES SIX

INGREDIENTS
  175ml/6fl oz/¾ cup salad oil,
    preferably olive oil
  115g/4oz/2 cups French or
    Italian bread, cut in 2.5cm/
    1in cubes
  1 large garlic clove, crushed with
    the flat side of a knife
  1 cos or romaine lettuce
  2 eggs, boiled for 1 minute
  120ml/4fl oz/½ cup
    lemon juice
  50g/2oz/⅔ cup freshly grated
    Parmesan cheese
  6 anchovy fillets, drained and
    finely chopped (optional)
  salt and ground black pepper

1 Heat 50ml/2fl oz/¼ cup of the oil in a frying pan. Add the bread and garlic and cook, stirring constantly, until the cubes are golden brown. Drain on kitchen paper and discard the garlic.

2 Tear large lettuce leaves into smaller pieces. Put all the lettuce in a bowl.

6 Sprinkle the croûtons on top of the salad and serve immediately.

COOK'S TIPS
To make a tangier dressing, mix the olive oil with 30ml/2 tbsp white wine vinegar, 2.5ml/½ tsp mustard, 5ml/1 tsp sugar, and salt and pepper.

Per portion: Energy 307Kcal/1272kJ; Protein 8g; Carbohydrate 11.7g, of which sugars 1.4g; Fat 25.7g, of which saturates 5.4g; Cholesterol 84mg; Calcium 149mg; Fibre 0.7g; Sodium 230mg.

WARM DRESSED SALAD WITH POACHED EGGS

SOFT POACHED EGGS, CHILLI, HOT CROÛTONS AND COOL, CRISP SALAD LEAVES MAKE A LIVELY AND UNUSUAL COMBINATION. THIS DELICIOUS SALAD IS PERFECT FOR A SUMMER LUNCH.

SERVES TWO

INGREDIENTS
½ small loaf Granary (whole-wheat) bread
45ml/3 tbsp chilli oil
2 eggs
115g/4oz mixed salad leaves
45ml/3 tbsp extra virgin olive oil
2 garlic cloves, crushed
15ml/1 tbsp balsamic vinegar
50g/2oz Parmesan cheese, shaved
ground black pepper (optional)

1 Carefully cut the crust from the Granary loaf and discard. Cut the bread into 2.5cm/1in cubes.

2 Heat the chilli oil in a large frying pan. Add the bread cubes and cook for about 5 minutes, tossing the cubes occasionally, until they are crisp and golden brown all over.

COOK'S TIP
If you are very sensitive to spicy flavours, cook the croûtons in olive oil or a nut oil, such as walnut or hazelnut, rather than using chilli oil.

3 Meanwhile, bring a pan of water to the boil. Break each egg into a jug (pitcher) and carefully slide into the water, one at a time. Gently poach the eggs for about 4 minutes until cooked.

4 Divide the salad leaves between two plates. Remove the croûtons from the pan and arrange them over the leaves.

5 Wipe the pan clean with kitchen paper. Then heat the olive oil in the pan, add the garlic and vinegar and cook over high heat for 1 minute. Pour the warm dressing over the salads.

6 Place a poached egg on each salad. Top with thin Parmesan shavings and a little ground black pepper, if you like.

Per portion: Energy 730Kcal/3042kJ; Protein 26.2g; Carbohydrate 48.4g, of which sugars 3.9g; Fat 49.3g, of which saturates 12.1g; Cholesterol 215mg; Calcium 556mg; Fibre 3.8g; Sodium 890mg.

PRAWN SALAD

IN MEXICO, THIS SALAD WOULD FORM THE FISH COURSE IN A FORMAL MEAL, BUT IT IS SO GOOD THAT YOU'LL WANT TO SERVE IT ON ALL SORTS OF OCCASIONS. IT IS PERFECT FOR A BUFFET LUNCH.

SERVES FOUR

INGREDIENTS
    450g/1lb cooked peeled
      prawns (shrimp)
    juice of 1 lime
    3 tomatoes
    1 ripe but firm avocado
    30ml/2 tbsp hot chilli sauce
    5ml/1 tsp sugar
    150ml/¼ pint/⅔ cup sour cream
    2 Little Gem (Bibb) lettuces
    salt and ground black pepper
    fresh basil leaves and strips of green
      (bell) pepper to garnish

1 Put the prawns in a large bowl, add the lime juice and salt and pepper. Toss lightly, then leave to marinate.

2 Cut a cross in the base of each tomato. Place them in a heatproof bowl and pour over boiling water to cover.

3 After 3 minutes, lift the tomatoes out on a slotted spoon and plunge them into a bowl of cold water. Drain. The skins will have begun to peel back easily from the crosses.

4 Peel the tomatoes completely, then cut them in half and squeeze out the seeds. Chop the flesh into 1cm/½in cubes and add it to the prawns.

5 Cut the avocado in half, remove the skin and stone (pit), then slice the flesh into 1cm/½in chunks. Add it to the prawn and tomato mixture.

6 Mix the hot chilli sauce, sugar and sour cream in a bowl. Fold into the prawn mixture. Line a bowl with the lettuce leaves, then top with the prawn mixture. Cover and chill for at least 1 hour, then garnish with fresh basil and strips of green pepper. Crusty bread makes a perfect accompaniment.

Per portion: Energy 284Kcal/1185kJ; Protein 28.1g; Carbohydrate 5g, of which sugars 4.4g; Fat 16.9g, of which saturates 6.7g; Cholesterol 114mg; Calcium 226mg; Fibre 2.3g; Sodium 1814mg.

SALAD NIÇOISE

MADE WITH THE FRESHEST OF INGREDIENTS, THIS CLASSIC PROVENÇAL SALAD MAKES A SIMPLE YET UNBEATABLE SUMMER DISH. SERVE WITH COUNTRY-STYLE BREAD AND CHILLED WHITE WINE.

SERVES FOUR

INGREDIENTS
  115g/4oz green beans, trimmed
    and cut in half
  115g/4oz mixed salad leaves
  ½ small cucumber, thinly sliced
  4 ripe tomatoes, quartered
  50g/2oz can anchovies, drained
  4 eggs, hard-boiled
  1 tuna steak, about 175g/6oz
  olive oil, for brushing
  ½ bunch of small radishes, trimmed
  50g/2oz/½ cup small
    black olives
  salt and ground black pepper
For the dressing
  90ml/6 tbsp extra virgin olive oil
  2 garlic cloves, crushed
  15ml/1 tbsp white wine vinegar

1 To make the dressing, whisk together the oil, garlic and vinegar in a bowl and season to taste with salt and pepper. Alternatively, shake together in a screw-top jar. Set aside.

2 Cook the green beans in a pan of boiling water for 2 minutes, until just tender, then drain.

3 Mix together the salad leaves, sliced cucumber, tomatoes and green beans in a large, shallow bowl. Halve the anchovies lengthways and shell and quarter the eggs.

VARIATION
Opinions vary on whether Salad Niçoise should include potatoes but, if you like, include a few small cooked new potatoes.

4 Preheat the grill (broiler). Brush the tuna with olive oil and sprinkle with salt and black pepper. Grill (broil) for 3–4 minutes on each side until cooked through. Cool, then flake with a fork.

5 Sprinkle the flaked tuna, sliced anchovies, quartered eggs, radishes and olives over the salad. Pour over the dressing and toss together lightly to combine. Serve immediately.

Per portion: Energy 378Kcal/1569kJ; Protein 23g; Carbohydrate 5.1g, of which sugars 4.7g; Fat 29.6g, of which saturates 5.2g; Cholesterol 241mg; Calcium 122mg; Fibre 2.5g; Sodium 889mg.

WARM SALAD WITH HAM, EGG AND ASPARAGUS

WHEN YOU THINK IT'S TOO HOT FOR PASTA, TRY SERVING IT IN A WARM SALAD. A MUSTARD DRESSING MADE FROM THE ASPARAGUS STEMS CREATES A RICH AND TANGY ACCOMPANIMENT.

SERVES FOUR

INGREDIENTS
    450g/1lb asparagus
    450g/1lb dried tagliatelle
    225g/8oz cooked ham, in 5mm/¼in
        thick slices, cut into sticks
    2 eggs, hard-boiled and sliced
    50g/2oz Parmesan cheese, shaved
    salt and ground black pepper
For the dressing
    50g/2oz cooked potato
    75ml/5 tbsp olive oil, preferably Sicilian
    15ml/1 tbsp lemon juice
    10ml/2 tsp Dijon mustard
    120ml/4fl oz/½ cup vegetable stock

VARIATIONS
Use sliced chicken instead of the ham or thin slices of softer Italian cheese, such as Fontina or asiago.

1 Trim and discard the tough woody part of the asparagus. Cut the spears in half and cook the thicker halves in boiling salted water for 12 minutes. After 6 minutes add the tips. Drain, then refresh under cold water until warm.

2 Finely chop 150g/5oz of the thick asparagus pieces. Place in a food processor with the dressing ingredients and process until smooth.

3 Cook the pasta in a large pan of salted water according to the packet instructions, until tender. Refresh under cold water until warm, and drain.

4 To serve, toss the pasta with the asparagus sauce and divide among four plates. Top with the ham, hard-boiled eggs and asparagus tips. Serve immediately with a sprinkling of Parmesan cheese shavings.

Per portion: Energy 707Kcal/2975kJ; Protein 36g; Carbohydrate 88.4g, of which sugars 6.6g; Fat 25.8g, of which saturates 6.4g; Cholesterol 159mg; Calcium 230mg; Fibre 5.3g; Sodium 859mg.

BEAN SALAD WITH TUNA AND RED ONION

THIS MAKES A GREAT, SUMMERY MAIN MEAL IF SERVED WITH A GREEN SALAD, SOME GARLIC MAYONNAISE AND PLENTY OF WARM, CRUSTY BREAD.

SERVES FOUR

INGREDIENTS

250g/9oz/1⅓ cups dried haricot
  (navy) or cannellini beans, soaked
  overnight in cold water
1 bay leaf
200–250g/7–9oz fine green
  beans, trimmed
1 large red onion, very thinly sliced
45ml/3 tbsp chopped fresh flat
  leaf parsley
200–250g/7–9oz good-quality canned
  tuna in olive oil, drained
200g/7oz cherry tomatoes, halved
salt and ground black pepper
a few onion rings, to garnish
For the dressing
  90ml/6 tbsp extra virgin olive oil
  15ml/1 tbsp tarragon vinegar
  5ml/1 tsp tarragon mustard
  1 garlic clove, finely chopped
  5ml/1 tsp grated lemon rind
  a little lemon juice
  pinch of caster (superfine)
    sugar (optional)

1 Drain the beans and bring them to the boil in fresh water with the bay leaf added. Boil rapidly for 10 minutes, then reduce the heat and boil steadily for 1–1½ hours, until tender. Drain well. Discard the bay leaf.

2 Meanwhile, place all the dressing ingredients apart from the lemon juice and sugar in a jug (pitcher) and whisk until mixed. Season to taste with salt, pepper, lemon juice and a pinch of caster sugar, if you like. Leave to stand.

3 Blanch the green beans in plenty of boiling water for 3–4 minutes. Drain, refresh under cold water and drain thoroughly again.

4 Place both types of beans in a bowl. Add half the dressing and toss to mix. Stir in the onion and half the chopped parsley, then season to taste with salt and pepper.

5 Flake the tuna into large chunks with a knife and toss it into the beans with the tomato halves.

6 Arrange the salad on four individual plates. Drizzle the remaining dressing over the salad and sprinkle the remaining chopped parsley on top. Garnish with a few onion rings and serve immediately, at room temperature.

Per portion: Energy 443Kcal/1857kJ; Protein 29.1g; Carbohydrate 33.7g, of which sugars 6.4g; Fat 22.3g, of which saturates 3.3g; Cholesterol 25mg; Calcium 100mg; Fibre 12g; Sodium 162mg.

Beef and Grilled Sweet Potato Salad with Shallot and Herb Dressing

This salad makes a good main dish for a summer buffet. It is absolutely delicious with a simple potato salad and some peppery leaves, such as watercress, mizuna or rocket.

3 Remove the beef from the oven, and cover with foil, then leave to rest for 10–15 minutes.

4 Meanwhile, preheat the grill (broiler). Cut the sweet potatoes into 1cm/½in slices. Brush with the remaining olive oil, season to taste with salt and pepper, and grill (broil) for about 5–6 minutes on each side, until tender and browned. Cut the sweet potato slices into strips and place them in a bowl.

5 Cut the beef into slices or strips and toss with the sweet potato, then set the bowl aside.

6 For the dressing, process the garlic, parsley, coriander, capers, chilli, mustard and 10ml/2 tsp of the vinegar in a food processor or blender until chopped. With the motor still running, gradually pour in the oil to make a smooth dressing. Season the dressing with salt and pepper and add more vinegar, to taste. Stir in the shallots.

7 Toss the dressing into the sweet potatoes and beef and leave to stand for up to 2 hours before serving.

SERVES SIX TO EIGHT

INGREDIENTS
  800g/1¾lb fillet (tenderloin) of beef
  5ml/1 tsp black peppercorns, crushed
  10ml/2 tsp chopped fresh thyme
  60ml/4 tbsp olive oil
  450g/1lb orange-fleshed sweet
    potato, peeled
  salt and ground black pepper
For the dressing
  1 garlic clove, chopped
  15g/½oz/½ cup flat leaf parsley
  30ml/2 tbsp chopped fresh
    coriander (cilantro)
  15ml/1 tbsp salted capers, rinsed
  ½–1 fresh green chilli, seeded
    and chopped
  10ml/2 tsp Dijon mustard
  10–15ml/2–3 tsp white wine vinegar
  75ml/5 tbsp extra virgin olive oil
  2 shallots, finely chopped

1 Roll the beef fillet in the crushed peppercorns and thyme, then set aside to marinate for a few hours. Preheat the oven to 200°C/400°F/Gas 6.

2 Heat half the olive oil in a heavy frying pan. Add the beef and brown it all over, turning frequently, to seal it. Place on a baking tray and cook in the oven for 10–15 minutes.

COOK'S TIP
Not only do orange-fleshed sweet potatoes look more appetizing than white ones, but they are also better for you, as they contain antioxidant vitamins that help protect against disease.

Per portion: Energy 400Kcal/1670kJ; Protein 29.2g; Carbohydrate 16g, of which sugars 4.3g; Fat 24.9g, of which saturates 6.2g; Cholesterol 81mg; Calcium 23mg; Fibre 1.8g; Sodium 89mg.

WARM CHICKEN <u>AND</u> TOMATO SALAD <u>WITH</u> HAZELNUT DRESSING

THIS SIMPLE, WARM SALAD COMBINES PAN-FRIED CHICKEN AND SPINACH WITH A LIGHT, NUTTY DRESSING. SERVE IT FOR LUNCH ON AN AUTUMN DAY.

SERVES FOUR

INGREDIENTS

   45ml/3 tbsp olive oil
   30ml/2 tbsp hazelnut oil
   15ml/1 tbsp white wine vinegar
   1 garlic clove, crushed
   15ml/1 tbsp chopped fresh mixed herbs
   225g/8oz baby spinach leaves
   250g/9oz cherry tomatoes, halved
   1 bunch of spring onions
    (scallions), chopped
   2 skinless chicken breast fillets, cut
    into thin strips
   salt and ground black pepper

VARIATIONS

• Use other meat or fish, such as steak, pork fillet (tenderloin) or salmon fillet, in place of the chicken.
• Any salad leaves can be used instead of the baby spinach.

1 First make the dressing: place 30ml/ 2 tbsp of the olive oil, the hazelnut oil, vinegar, garlic and chopped herbs in a small bowl or jug (pitcher) and whisk together until mixed. Set aside.

2 Trim any long stalks from the spinach leaves, then place in a large serving bowl with the tomatoes and spring onions, and toss together to mix.

3 Heat the remaining olive oil in a frying pan, and stir-fry the chicken over a high heat for 7–10 minutes, until it is cooked, tender and lightly browned.

4 Arrange the cooked chicken pieces over the salad. Give the dressing a quick whisk to blend, then drizzle it over the salad. Add salt and pepper to taste, toss lightly and serve immediately.

Per portion: Energy 234Kcal/973kJ; Protein 20.5g; Carbohydrate 3.6g, of which sugars 3.5g; Fat 15.3g, of which saturates 2.4g; Cholesterol 53mg; Calcium 114mg; Fibre 2.2g; Sodium 131mg.

POTATO AND RED PEPPER FRITTATA

A frittata is like a large omelette. This tasty version is filled with potatoes and plenty of herbs. Do use fresh mint in preference to dried if you can find it.

2 Whisk together the eggs, mint and seasoning in a bowl, then set aside. Heat the oil in a large frying pan.

3 Add the onion, garlic, peppers and potatoes to the pan and cook, stirring occasionally, for 5 minutes.

4 Pour the egg mixture over the vegetables in the frying pan and stir gently over a low heat.

5 Push the mixture towards the centre of the pan as it cooks to allow the liquid egg to run on to the base. Meanwhile preheat the grill (broiler).

6 When the frittata is lightly set, place the pan under the hot grill for 2–3 minutes until the top is a light golden brown colour.

7 Serve hot or cold, cut into wedges piled high on a serving dish and garnished with sprigs of mint.

SERVES THREE TO FOUR

INGREDIENTS
    450g/1lb small new or
      salad potatoes
    6 eggs
    30ml/2 tbsp chopped
      fresh mint
    30ml/2 tbsp olive oil
    1 onion, chopped
    2 garlic cloves, crushed
    2 red (bell) peppers, seeded and
      coarsely chopped
    salt and ground black pepper
    fresh mint sprigs,
      to garnish

1 Cook the potatoes in their skins in lightly salted, boiling water until just tender. Drain and leave to cool slightly, then cut into thick slices.

Per portion: Energy 374Kcal/1563kJ; Protein 16.7g; Carbohydrate 34.9g, of which sugars 11.3g; Fat 19.4g, of which saturates 4.5g; Cholesterol 381mg; Calcium 87mg; Fibre 3.9g; Sodium 162mg.

FRITTATA WITH LEEK AND SPINACH

ITALIAN FRITTATA IS SIMILAR TO SPANISH TORTILLA. THIS COMBINATION OF SWEET LEEK, RED PEPPER AND SPINACH IS WONDERFULLY DELICIOUS WITH THE EGG.

SERVES THREE TO FOUR

INGREDIENTS
    30ml/2 tbsp olive oil
    1 red (bell) pepper, seeded and diced
    2.5–5ml/½–1 tsp ground
      toasted cumin
    3 leeks (about 450g/1lb),
      thinly sliced
    150g/5oz small spinach leaves
    45ml/3 tbsp pine nuts, toasted
    5 large (US extra large) eggs
    15ml/1 tbsp chopped fresh basil
    15ml/1 tbsp chopped fresh flat
      leaf parsley
    salt and ground black pepper
    watercress, to garnish
    50g/2oz/⅔ cup grated Parmesan
      cheese, to serve (optional)

1 Heat a frying pan and add the oil. Add the red pepper and cook over a medium heat, stirring occasionally, for 6–8 minutes, until soft and beginning to brown. Add 2.5ml/½ tsp of the cumin and cook for another 1–2 minutes.

2 Stir in the leeks, then part-cover the pan and cook gently for about 5 minutes, until the leeks have softened and collapsed. Season with salt and ground black pepper.

3 Add the spinach and cover. Leave the spinach to wilt in the steam for 3–4 minutes, then stir to mix it into the vegetables, adding the pine nuts.

4 Beat the eggs with salt, pepper, the remaining cumin, basil and parsley. Add to the pan and cook over a gentle heat until the bottom of the omelette sets and turns golden brown. Pull the edges of the omelette away from the sides of the pan as it cooks and tilt the pan so that the uncooked egg runs underneath.

5 Preheat the grill (broiler). Flash the frittata under the hot grill to set the egg on top, but do not let it become too brown.

6 Cut the frittata into wedges and serve warm, garnished with watercress and sprinkled with Parmesan, if using.

VARIATION
A delicious way to serve frittata is to pack it into a slightly hollowed-out crusty loaf and then drizzle it with a little extra virgin olive oil. Wrap tightly in clear film (plastic wrap) and leave to stand for 1–2 hours before cutting into thick slices. It is ideal picnic fare.

Per portion: Energy 268Kcal/1115kJ; Protein 15.5g; Carbohydrate 9.3g, of which sugars 8g; Fat 19g, of which saturates 2g; Cholesterol 0mg; Calcium 132mg; Fibre 5.5g; Sodium 265mg.

SOFT TACOS WITH SPICED OMELETTE

SERVED HOT, WARM OR COLD, THESE TACOS MAKE EASY FOOD ON THE MOVE FOR YOUNGER MEMBERS OF THE FAMILY, WHEN THEY NEED SOMETHING NOURISHING TO TAKE ON A PICNIC, HIKE OR CYCLE RIDE.

SERVES FOUR

INGREDIENTS
   30ml/2 tbsp sunflower oil
   50g/2oz/1 cup beansprouts
   50g/2oz carrots, cut into
      thin sticks
   25g/1oz Chinese cabbage, chopped
   15ml/1 tbsp light soy sauce
   4 eggs
   1 small spring onion (scallion),
      thinly sliced
   5ml/1 tsp Cajun seasoning
   25g/1oz/2 tbsp butter
   4 soft flour tortillas, warmed in
      the oven or microwave
   salt and ground black pepper

COOK'S TIP
You can buy fresh soft tortillas in large supermarkets. They freeze well, so keep a packet or two in the freezer.

1 Heat the oil in a small frying pan and stir-fry the beansprouts, carrot sticks and chopped cabbage until they begin to soften. Add the soy sauce, stir to combine and set aside.

2 Place the eggs, sliced spring onion, Cajun seasoning, salt and ground black pepper in a bowl, and beat together. Melt the butter in a small pan until it sizzles. Add the beaten eggs and cook over a gentle heat, stirring constantly, until almost firm.

3 Divide the vegetables and scrambled egg evenly among the tortillas, fold up into cones or parcels and serve. For travelling, the tacos can be wrapped in kitchen paper and foil.

VARIATION
Fill warm pitta breads with this spicy omelette mixture. Mini pitta breads are perfect for younger children who may find the folded tacos difficult to handle.

FRENCH COUNTRY-STYLE EGGS

THIS VARIATION ON AN OMELETTE COOKS THE "FILLING" IN THE OMELETTE MIXTURE ITSELF. YOU CAN INCORPORATE LOTS OF DIFFERENT INGREDIENTS, SUCH AS LEFTOVER VEGETABLES.

SERVES TWO

INGREDIENTS
   45–75ml/3–5 tbsp sunflower oil
   50g/2oz thick bacon rashers (strips)
      or pieces, rinds removed
      and chopped
   2 thick slices of bread,
      cut into small cubes
   1 small onion, chopped
   1–2 celery sticks, thinly sliced
   115g/4oz cooked potato, diced
   5 eggs, beaten
   2 garlic cloves, crushed
   handful of young spinach or sorrel
      leaves, stalks removed,
      torn into pieces
   few fresh parsley sprigs, chopped
   salt and ground black pepper

1 Heat the oil in a large heavy frying pan, and cook the bacon and bread cubes until they are crisp and turning golden. Add the chopped onion, celery and diced potato, and continue cooking over a low heat, stirring frequently until all the vegetables have softened and are beginning to turn golden brown.

2 Beat the eggs with the garlic and seasoning, and pour over the vegetables. When the underside is beginning to set, add the spinach or sorrel. Cook until they have wilted and the omelette is only just soft in the middle. Fold the omelette in half and slide it out of the pan. Serve topped with the parsley, if you like.

Top per portion: Energy 280Kcal/1168kJ; Protein 9.5g; Carbohydrate 24.2g, of which sugars 2g; Fat 16.7g, of which saturates 5.5g; Cholesterol 204mg; Calcium 80mg; Fibre 1.5g; Sodium 217mg.
Below per portion: Energy 488Kcal/2034kJ; Protein 23.7g; Carbohydrate 26.2g, of which sugars 3.4g; Fat 32.7g, of which saturates 6.7g; Cholesterol 483mg; Calcium 130mg; Fibre 2.1g; Sodium 649mg.

SOUFFLÉ OMELETTE <u>WITH</u> MUSHROOMS

A LIGHT-AS-AIR OMELETTE MAKES AN IDEAL MEAL FOR ONE, ESPECIALLY WITH THIS DELICIOUS FILLING. USE A COMBINATION OF DIFFERENT MUSHROOMS IF YOU LIKE.

SERVES ONE

INGREDIENTS
 2 eggs, separated
 15g/½oz/1 tbsp butter
 flat leaf parsley or coriander
  (cilantro) leaves, to garnish
For the mushroom sauce
 15g/½oz/1 tbsp butter
 75g/3oz/generous 1 cup button
  (white) mushrooms, thinly sliced
 15ml/1 tbsp plain (all-purpose) flour
 85–120ml/3–4fl oz/⅓–½ cup milk
 5ml/1 tsp chopped fresh
  parsley (optional)
 salt and ground black pepper

1 To make the mushroom sauce, melt the butter in a pan or frying pan and add the sliced mushrooms. Cook gently for 4–5 minutes, stirring occasionally, until tender and golden.

2 Stir in the flour, then gradually add the milk, stirring constantly. Cook until boiling and thickened. Add the parsley, if using, and season to taste with salt and pepper. Keep warm.

3 Beat the egg yolks with 15ml/1 tbsp water and season with a little salt and pepper. Whisk the egg whites until stiff, then fold into the egg yolks using a metal spoon. Preheat the grill (broiler).

4 Melt the butter in a large frying pan and pour the egg mixture into the pan. Cook over a gentle heat for 2–4 minutes. Place the frying pan under the grill and cook for a further 3–4 minutes until the top is golden brown.

5 Slide the omelette on to a warmed serving plate, pour the mushroom sauce over the top and fold the omelette in half. Serve, garnished with parsley or coriander leaves.

COOK'S TIP
For extra flavour, add a few drops of Worcestershire sauce to the mushrooms as they are cooking.

Per portion: Energy 566Kcal/2348kJ; Protein 18.9g; Carbohydrate 20.1g, of which sugars 4.7g; Fat 46.1g, of which saturates 25g; Cholesterol 471mg; Calcium 199mg; Fibre 1.4g; Sodium 423mg.

OMELETTE ARNOLD BENNETT

CREATED FOR THE AUTHOR ARNOLD BENNETT, WHO FREQUENTLY DINED AT THE SAVOY HOTEL IN LONDON, THIS CREAMY, SMOKED HADDOCK SOUFFLÉ OMELETTE IS NOW SERVED ALL OVER THE WORLD.

SERVES TWO

INGREDIENTS

175g/6oz smoked haddock fillet, poached and drained
50g/2oz/4 tbsp butter, diced
175ml/6fl oz/¾ cup whipping or double (heavy) cream
4 eggs, separated
40g/1½oz/⅓ cup grated mature (sharp) Cheddar cheese
ground black pepper
watercress, to garnish

COOK'S TIP

Try to buy traditional cold-smoked haddock that does not contain artificial colouring for this recipe. Besides being better for you, it gives the omelette a lighter, more attractive colour.

1 Remove the skin and any bones from the haddock fillet and discard. Carefully flake the flesh using a fork.

2 Melt half the butter with 60ml/4 tbsp of the cream in a fairly small non-stick pan, then add the flaked fish and stir together gently. Cover the pan with a lid, remove it from the heat and set aside to cool completely.

3 Mix the egg yolks with 15ml/1 tbsp cream. Add pepper, then stir into the fish. In a separate bowl, mix the cheese and the remaining cream. Stiffly whisk the egg whites, then fold into the fish mixture. Heat the remaining butter in an omelette pan, add the fish mixture and cook until browned underneath. Pour the cheese mixture over and grill (broil) until bubbling. Garnish and serve.

Per portion: Energy 821Kcal/3396kJ; Protein 36.1g; Carbohydrate 2.6g, of which sugars 2.6g; Fat 74g, of which saturates 42.6g; Cholesterol 577mg; Calcium 280mg; Fibre 0g; Sodium 1123mg.

RICE, RISOTTO, PASTA & NOODLES

Risottos are perfect if you enjoy chatting to friends and family while you prepare the meal, as you need to stand at the stove and constantly stir until the rice is cooked – but the results are worth waiting for. Stuffed Vegetables and Basmati and Nut Pilaff are two other dishes ideal for entertaining. Like the delicious Seafood Lasagne, they are full of flavour and the combination of ingredients means that every aromatic mouthful brings an unexpected delight. For a more unusual treat, try Sichuan Noodles with Sesame Sauce, or give your tastebuds a tingle with Burritos with Chicken and Rice.

STUFFED VEGETABLES

THIS MAKES A POPULAR SUPPER DISH, AND WITH A CHOICE OF VEGETABLES INCLUDED IN THE RECIPE, THERE'S BOUND TO BE SOMETHING TO APPEAL TO EVERY MEMBER OF THE FAMILY.

SERVES FOUR

INGREDIENTS
  1 aubergine (eggplant)
  1 green (bell) pepper
  2 beefsteak tomatoes
  45ml/3 tbsp olive oil
  1 onion, chopped
  2 garlic cloves, crushed
  115g/4oz/1–1½ cups button (white)
    mushrooms, chopped
  1 carrot, grated
  225g/8oz/2 cups cooked white long
    grain rice
  15ml/1 tbsp chopped fresh dill
  90g/3½oz/scant ½ cup crumbled
    feta cheese
  75g/3oz/¾ cup pine nuts,
    lightly toasted
  30ml/2 tbsp currants
  salt and ground black pepper

1 Preheat the oven to 190°C/375°F/ Gas 5. Lightly grease a shallow ovenproof dish. Cut the aubergine in half, through the stalk, and scoop out the flesh from each half, taking care not to pierce the skin, to leave two hollow "boats". Dice the aubergine flesh. Cut the pepper in half lengthways and remove the cores and seeds.

2 Cut off the tops from the tomatoes and hollow out the centres with a spoon. Chop the flesh and add it to the diced aubergine. Place the tomatoes upside down on kitchen paper to drain.

3 Bring a pan of water to the boil, add the aubergine halves and blanch for 3 minutes. Add the pepper halves to the boiling water and blanch for 3 minutes more. Drain the vegetables, then place, hollow side up, in the baking dish.

4 Heat 30ml/2 tbsp oil in a pan and cook the onion and garlic for about 5 minutes. Stir in the diced aubergine and tomato mixture with the mushrooms and carrot. Cover, cook for 5 minutes until softened, then mix in the rice, dill, feta, pine nuts and currants. Season to taste.

5 Divide the mixture among the vegetable shells, sprinkle with the remaining olive oil and bake for 20 minutes, until the topping has browned. Serve hot or cold.

Per portion: Energy 544Kcal/2265kJ; Protein 12.9g; Carbohydrate 63.3g, of which sugars 17.2g; Fat 26.8g, of which saturates 5.3g; Cholesterol 16mg; Calcium 134mg; Fibre 4.1g; Sodium 343mg.

BASMATI AND NUT PILAFF

VEGETARIANS WILL LOVE THIS SIMPLE PILAFF. IT IS STRAIGHTFORWARD TO MAKE, YET IT IS FULL OF DELICIOUS INDIAN FLAVOURS. ADD WILD OR CULTIVATED MUSHROOMS, IF YOU LIKE.

SERVES FOUR

INGREDIENTS

15–30ml/1–2 tbsp sunflower oil
1 onion, chopped
1 garlic clove, crushed
1 large carrot, coarsely grated
225g/8oz/generous 1 cup basmati
 rice, soaked
5ml/1 tsp cumin seeds
10ml/2 tsp ground coriander
10ml/2 tsp black mustard
 seeds (optional)
4 green cardamom pods
450ml/¾ pint/scant 2 cups vegetable
 stock or water
1 bay leaf
75g/3oz/¾ cup unsalted walnuts and
 cashew nuts
salt and ground black pepper
fresh parsley or coriander (cilantro)
 sprigs, to garnish

1 Heat the oil in a large, shallow frying pan. Add the onion, garlic and carrot and cook over a low heat, stirring occasionally, for 3–4 minutes, until softened. Thoroughly drain the rice and then add to the pan with the cumin seeds, ground coriander, black mustard seeds and cardamom pods. Cook for 1–2 minutes more, stirring constantly to coat the grains in oil.

2 Pour in the stock or water, add the bay leaf and season well. Bring to the boil, lower the heat, cover and simmer very gently for 10–12 minutes.

3 Remove the pan from the heat without lifting the lid. Leave to stand for about 5 minutes, then check the rice. If it is cooked, there will be small steam holes on the surface of the rice. Remove and discard the bay leaf and the cardamom pods.

4 Stir in the nuts, taste and adjust the seasoning if necessary. Spoon on to a warm platter, garnish with the parsley or coriander and serve.

COOK'S TIP
Use whichever nuts you prefer in this dish – even unsalted peanuts taste good, although almonds, cashew nuts or pistachios are more exotic.

Per portion: Energy 376Kcal/1562kJ; Protein 7.5g; Carbohydrate 50g, of which sugars 4g; Fat 16g, of which saturates 1.4g; Cholesterol 0mg; Calcium 43mg; Fibre 1.6g; Sodium 7mg.

RISOTTO WITH FOUR CHEESES

THIS MAKES AN EXCELLENT AND COLOURFUL VEGETARIAN LUNCH OR SUPPER DISH.

SERVES FOUR

INGREDIENTS
40g/1½oz/3 tbsp butter
1 small onion, finely chopped
1.2 litres/2 pints/5 cups chicken
  stock, preferably home-made
350g/12oz/1¾ cups risotto rice
200ml/7fl oz/scant 1 cup dry
  white wine
50g/2oz/½ cup grated Gruyère cheese
50g/2oz/½ cup diced taleggio cheese
50g/2oz/½ cup diced
  Gorgonzola cheese
50g/2oz/⅔ cup freshly grated
  Parmesan cheese
salt and ground black pepper
chopped fresh flat leaf parsley,
  to garnish

1 Melt the butter in a large, heavy pan or deep frying pan and cook the onion over a low heat, stirring frequently, for about 4–5 minutes, until softened and lightly browned. Meanwhile, pour the chicken stock into another pan and heat it to simmering point.

2 Add the rice to the onion mixture, stir until the grains start to swell and burst, then add the wine. Stir until it stops sizzling and most of it has been absorbed by the rice, then pour in a little of the hot stock. Add salt and pepper to taste. Stir over a low heat until the stock has been absorbed.

3 Gradually add the remaining stock, a little at a time, allowing the rice to absorb the liquid before adding more, and stirring constantly. After about 20–25 minutes the rice will be *al dente* and the risotto creamy.

4 Turn off the heat under the pan, then add the Gruyère, taleggio, Gorgonzola and 30ml/2 tbsp of the Parmesan cheese. Stir gently until the cheeses have melted, then taste and adjust the seasoning, if necessary. Spoon the risotto into a warm serving bowl and garnish with parsley. Serve immediately, handing the remaining grated Parmesan separately.

Per portion: Energy 640Kcal/2662kJ; Protein 22.1g; Carbohydrate 67.1g, of which sugars 1.2g; Fat 26g, of which saturates 15.9g; Cholesterol 70mg; Calcium 451mg; Fibre 0.2g; Sodium 473mg.

RISOTTO WITH FOUR VEGETABLES

THIS IS ONE OF THE PRETTIEST RISOTTOS, ESPECIALLY WHEN MADE WITH ACORN SQUASH.

SERVES THREE TO FOUR

INGREDIENTS
115g/4oz/1 cup shelled fresh peas
115g/4oz/1 cup green beans, cut
  into short lengths
30ml/2 tbsp olive oil
75g/3oz/6 tbsp butter
1 acorn squash, skin and seeds
  removed, flesh cut into batons
1 onion, finely chopped
275g/10oz/1½ cups risotto rice
120ml/4fl oz/½ cup Italian dry
  white vermouth
1 litre/1¾ pints/4 cups boiling
  chicken stock
75g/3oz/1 cup freshly grated
  Parmesan cheese
salt and ground black pepper

1 Bring a pan of lightly salted water to the boil, add the peas and beans and cook for 2–3 minutes, until the vegetables are just tender. Drain, refresh under cold running water, drain again and set aside.

2 Heat the oil with 25g/1oz/2 tbsp of the butter in a medium pan until foaming. Add the squash and cook gently for 2–3 minutes, or until just softened. Remove with a slotted spoon and set aside. Add the onion to the pan and cook gently for about 3 minutes, stirring frequently, until softened.

3 Stir in the rice until the grains start to swell and burst, then add the vermouth. Stir until the vermouth stops sizzling and most of it has been absorbed by the rice, then add a few ladlefuls of the stock, with salt and pepper to taste. Stir over a low heat until the stock has been absorbed.

4 Gradually add the remaining stock, a few ladlefuls at a time, allowing the rice to absorb the liquid before adding more, and stirring all the time.

VARIATIONS
Shelled broad (fava) beans can be used instead of the peas, and asparagus tips instead of the green beans. Use courgettes (zucchini) if acorn squash is not available.

5 After about 20 minutes, when all the stock has been absorbed and the rice is cooked and creamy but still has a "bite", gently stir in the vegetables, the remaining butter and about half the grated Parmesan. Heat through, then taste and adjust the seasoning and serve with the remaining grated Parmesan handed around separately.

Per portion: Energy 836Kcal/3472kJ; Protein 22.1g; Carbohydrate 79.4g, of which sugars 6g; Fat 42.6g, of which saturates 22.1g; Cholesterol 89mg; Calcium 379mg; Fibre 3.9g; Sodium 462mg.

ROASTED PEPPER RISOTTO

THIS IS A VERY RICH DISH. IT IS THE PERFECT CHOICE FOR A DINNER PARTY WITH AN ITALIAN THEME, SERVED WITH A LIGHT, DRY SPARKLING WHITE WINE.

SERVES THREE TO FOUR

INGREDIENTS

 1 red (bell) pepper
 1 yellow (bell) pepper
 15ml/1 tbsp olive oil
 25g/1oz/2 tbsp butter
 1 onion, chopped
 2 garlic cloves, crushed
 275g/10oz/1½ cups risotto rice
 1 litre/1¾ pints/4 cups simmering
   vegetable stock
 50g/2oz/⅔ cup freshly grated
   Parmesan cheese
 salt and ground black pepper
 freshly grated Parmesan cheese, to
   serve (optional)

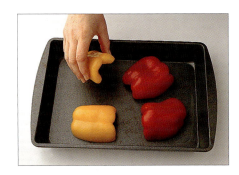

1 Preheat the grill (broiler). Cut the peppers in half, remove the seeds and pith and arrange, cut side down, on a baking sheet. Place under the grill for 5–6 minutes until the skin is charred. Put the peppers in a plastic bag, tie the ends and leave for 4–5 minutes.

2 Peel the peppers when they are cool enough to handle and the steam has loosened the skin. Cut into thin strips.

3 Heat the oil and butter in a pan and cook the onion and garlic for 4–5 minutes over a low heat until the onion begins to soften. Add the peppers and cook the mixture for 3–4 minutes more, stirring occasionally.

4 Stir in the rice. Cook over a medium heat for 3–4 minutes, stirring all the time, until the rice is evenly coated in oil and the outer part of each grain has become translucent.

5 Add a ladleful of stock. Cook, stirring, until all the liquid has been absorbed. Continue to add the stock, a ladleful at a time, making sure each quantity has been absorbed before adding the next.

6 When the rice is tender but retains a little "bite", stir in the Parmesan, and add seasoning to taste. Cover and leave to stand for 3–4 minutes, then serve, with extra Parmesan, if using.

Per portion: Energy 555Kcal/2312kJ; Protein 16.1g; Carbohydrate 80.1g, of which sugars 10g; Fat 18g, of which saturates 8.4g; Cholesterol 34mg; Calcium 238mg; Fibre 2.6g; Sodium 241mg.

KEDGEREE

THIS CLASSIC DISH ORIGINATED IN INDIA. IT IS BEST MADE WITH BASMATI RICE, WHICH GOES WELL WITH THE MILD CURRY FLAVOUR, BUT LONG GRAIN RICE WILL DO.

SERVES FOUR

INGREDIENTS

450g/1lb undyed smoked
   haddock fillet
750ml/1¼ pints/3 cups milk
2 bay leaves
½ lemon, sliced
50g/2oz/¼ cup butter
1 onion, chopped
2.5ml/½ tsp ground turmeric
5ml/1 tsp mild Madras curry powder
2 green cardamom pods
350g/12oz/1¾ cups basmati or long
   grain rice, washed and drained
4 hard-boiled eggs (not *too* hard),
   coarsely chopped
150ml/¼ pint/⅔ cup single (light)
   cream (optional)
30ml/2 tbsp chopped fresh parsley
salt and ground black pepper

1 Put the haddock in a shallow pan and add the milk, bay leaves and lemon slices. Poach gently for 8–10 minutes, until the haddock flakes easily when tested with the tip of a sharp knife. Strain the milk into a jug (pitcher), discarding the bay leaves and lemon slices. Remove the skin from the haddock and flake the flesh into large pieces. Keep hot until required.

2 Melt the butter in the pan, add the onion and cook over a low heat for about 3 minutes, until softened. Stir in the turmeric, the curry powder and cardamom pods and cook for 1 minute.

3 Add the rice, stirring to coat it well with the butter. Pour in the reserved milk, stir and bring to the boil. Lower the heat and simmer the rice for 10–12 minutes, until all the milk has been absorbed and the rice is tender. Season to taste, going easy on the salt.

4 Gently stir in the fish and hard-boiled eggs, with the cream, if using. Sprinkle with the parsley and serve.

VARIATION
Use smoked or poached fresh salmon for a delicious change from haddock.

Per portion: Energy 579Kcal/2421kJ; Protein 34.4g; Carbohydrate 71.1g, of which sugars 0.9g; Fat 17g, of which saturates 8.2g; Cholesterol 257mg; Calcium 76mg; Fibre 0.2g; Sodium 1001mg.

BURRITOS WITH CHICKEN AND RICE

IN MEXICO, BURRITOS ARE A POPULAR STREET FOOD, EATEN ON THE HOOF. THE SECRET OF A SUCCESSFUL BURRITO IS TO HAVE ALL THE FILLING NEATLY PACKAGED INSIDE THE TORTILLA FOR EASY EATING, SO THESE SNACKS ARE SELDOM SERVED WITH A POUR-OVER SAUCE.

SERVES FOUR

INGREDIENTS

90g/3½oz/½ cup long grain rice
15ml/1 tbsp vegetable oil
1 onion, chopped
2.5ml/½ tsp ground cloves
5ml/1 tsp dried, or fresh oregano
200g/7oz can chopped tomatoes
2 skinless, chicken breast fillets
150g/5oz/1¼ cups grated Monterey
  Jack or mild Cheddar cheese
60ml/4 tbsp sour cream (optional)
8 x 20–25cm/8–10in fresh wheat
  flour tortillas
salt
fresh oregano, to garnish (optional)

1 Bring a pan of lightly salted water to the boil. Add the rice, bring back to the boil and cook for 8 minutes. Drain, rinse and then drain again.

2 Heat the oil in a large pan. Add the onion, with the ground cloves and oregano, and cook, stirring occasionally, for 2–3 minutes. Stir in the rice and tomatoes, with their can juice, and cook over a low heat until all the tomato juice has been absorbed. Remove the pan from the heat and set aside.

3 Put the chicken fillets in a large pan, pour in enough water to cover and bring to the boil. Lower the heat and simmer for about 10 minutes, or until the chicken is cooked through. Lift the chicken out of the pan, put on a plate and leave to cool slightly.

4 Preheat the oven to 160°C/325°F/ Gas 3. Shred the chicken by pulling the flesh apart with two forks, then add the chicken to the rice mixture, with the grated cheese. Gently stir in the sour cream, if using.

5 Wrap the tortillas in foil and place them on a plate. Stand the plate over boiling water for about 5 minutes. Alternatively, wrap in microwave-safe film and heat in a microwave on full power for 1 minute.

6 Spoon one-eighth of the filling into the centre of a tortilla and fold in both sides. Fold the bottom up and the top down to form a parcel. Secure with a cocktail stick (toothpick).

7 Put the filled burrito in a shallow dish or casserole, cover with foil and keep warm in the oven while you make seven more. Remove the cocktail sticks before serving, sprinkled with fresh oregano.

VARIATION
For an extra touch of spice, you can add 3–4 canned or bottled jalapeño chillies to the filling, with the chicken, and substitute fresh coriander (cilantro) for the oregano. Rinse, seed and finely chopped the chillies first.

COOK'S TIP
If you use very fresh tortillas, you may be able to dispense with the cocktail sticks. Secure the tortilla parcels by damping the final fold with a little water. When you lay the burritos in the dish, place them with the folded surfaces down.

Per portion: Energy 625Kcal/2628kJ; Protein 37.4g; Carbohydrate 82.2g, of which sugars 4.6g; Fat 17.1g, of which saturates 8.7g; Cholesterol 89mg; Calcium 411mg; Fibre 3.3g; Sodium 617mg.

Pasta with Garlic and Chilli

This is the simplest of pasta dishes and one of the best. Mint and oregano give very different results, both good. There is no need to serve grated Parmesan with this dish — instead, let the clear flavour of the garlic and olive oil sing out.

SERVES THREE TO FOUR

INGREDIENTS

400g/14oz dried spaghetti
105ml/7 tbsp extra virgin olive oil, plus extra to taste
1.5ml/¼ tsp dried red chilli flakes or 2 small whole dried red chillies
6 large garlic cloves, finely chopped
15ml/1 tbsp chopped fresh mint or oregano
15g/½ oz chopped fresh flat leaf parsley
salt and ground black pepper

1 Cook the spaghetti in lightly salted, boiling water for 9–11 minutes, or according to the packet instructions, until just tender.

2 Meanwhile, heat the oil in a large frying pan or pan over a very gentle heat. Add the chilli flakes or whole chillies and cook very gently for 2–3 minutes.

COOK'S TIP
If you use fresh spaghetti, cook for only 2–3 minutes in salted, boiling water.

3 Add the garlic to the pan. Keep the heat very low, so that the garlic barely bubbles and does not brown, then cook, shaking the pan occasionally, for about 2 minutes. Remove the pan from the heat and cool a little, then add the fresh mint or oregano.

4 Drain the pasta, then immediately add it to the oil and garlic mixture, with the parsley. Toss thoroughly. Season with freshly ground black pepper and transfer to warmed serving bowls. Serve immediately, offering more olive oil for drizzling at the table.

VARIATION
Cook 250g/9oz broccoli florets in salted, boiling water for 4 minutes. Add to the chilli oil and cook for 5–8 minutes.

Per portion: Energy 688Kcal/2897kJ; Protein 16.2g; Carbohydrate 98.9g, of which sugars 4.5g; Fat 28.1g, of which saturates 3.9g; Cholesterol 0mg; Calcium 43mg; Fibre 4.1g; Sodium 6mg.

RIGATONI WITH TOMATOES AND FRESH HERBS

THIS PRETTY AND COLOURFUL PASTA DISH RELIES FOR ITS SUCCESS ON THE BEST ITALIAN CANNED TOMATOES AND TENDER YOUNG HERBS, FRESHLY PICKED. FOR A REAL TREAT, USE FRESH TOMATOES, PEELED AND PURÉED. ADD A LITTLE SUGAR IF THE TOMATOES ARE NOT AT THE PEAK OF RIPENESS.

SERVES SIX TO EIGHT

INGREDIENTS

1 onion
1 carrot
1 celery stick
60ml/4 tbsp olive oil
1 garlic clove, thinly sliced
a few leaves each of fresh basil,
  thyme and oregano or marjoram
2 x 400g/14oz cans chopped Italian
  plum tomatoes
15ml/1 tbsp sun-dried tomato paste
5ml/1 tsp granulated sugar
about 90ml/6 tbsp dry red or white
  wine (optional)
350g/12oz/3 cups dried rigatoni
salt and ground black pepper
coarsely shaved Parmesan cheese,
  to serve

COOK'S TIP
Large pasta tubes are best for this recipe, as they capture the wonderful tomato and herb sauce. If you can't get rigatoni, try penne or penne rigate (ridged penne).

1 Chop the onion, carrot and celery stick finely, either in a food processor or by hand, with a sharp knife.

2 Heat the olive oil in a medium pan, add the garlic slices and stir over a very low heat for 1–2 minutes. Do not let the garlic burn or it will taste bitter.

3 Add the chopped vegetables and the fresh herbs, reserving a few to garnish. Cook over a low heat, stirring frequently, for 5–7 minutes, until the vegetables have softened and are lightly coloured.

4 Add the canned tomatoes, tomato paste and sugar, then stir in the wine, if using. Add salt and pepper to taste. Bring to the boil, stirring, then lower the heat to a gentle simmer. Cook, stirring frequently, for about 45 minutes.

5 Cook the pasta in lightly salted, boiling water for 10–12 minutes, drain and tip into a warmed bowl. Pour the sauce over the pasta and toss well. Garnish with the reserved herbs. Serve immediately, with shavings of Parmesan handed separately.

Per portion: Energy 313Kcal/1323kJ; Protein 8.8g; Carbohydrate 51g, of which sugars 8.8g; Fat 8.6g, of which saturates 1.2g; Cholesterol 0mg; Calcium 43mg; Fibre 3.3g; Sodium 62mg.

SPAGHETTI WITH EGGS, BACON AND CREAM

*THIS ITALIAN CLASSIC, FLAVOURED WITH PANCETTA AND A GARLIC AND EGG SAUCE THAT COOKS
AROUND THE HOT SPAGHETTI, IS POPULAR WORLDWIDE. IT MAKES A GREAT LAST-MINUTE SUPPER.*

SERVES FOUR

INGREDIENTS
30ml/2 tbsp olive oil
1 small onion, finely chopped
1 large garlic clove, crushed
8 pancetta or rindless smoked
    streaky (fatty) bacon rashers
    (strips), cut into 1cm/½in strips
350g/12oz fresh or dried spaghetti
4 eggs
90–120ml/6–8 tbsp/½ cup
    crème fraîche
60ml/4 tbsp freshly grated
    Parmesan cheese, plus extra
    to serve
salt and ground black pepper

1 Heat the oil in a large pan, add the onion and garlic and cook gently for about 5 minutes, until softened.

2 Add the pancetta or bacon to the pan and cook for 10 minutes, stirring.

3 Meanwhile, cook the spaghetti in a large pan of salted, boiling water according to the instructions on the packet until *al dente*.

4 Put the eggs, crème fraîche and grated Parmesan in a bowl. Stir in plenty of black pepper, then beat together well.

5 Drain the pasta thoroughly, tip it into the pan with the pancetta or bacon and toss well to mix.

6 Turn off the heat under the pan, then immediately add the egg mixture and toss thoroughly so that it cooks lightly and coats the pasta.

7 Season to taste, then divide the spaghetti among four warmed bowls and sprinkle with freshly ground black pepper. Serve immediately, with extra grated Parmesan handed separately.

COOK'S TIP
You can replace the crème fraîche with either double (heavy) cream or sour cream, if you like.

Per portion: Energy 686Kcal/2873kJ; Protein 31.1g; Carbohydrate 66.6g, of which sugars 4.2g; Fat 34.5g, of which saturates 14.8g; Cholesterol 213mg; Calcium 243mg; Fibre 2.8g; Sodium 1098mg.

PASTA WITH TOMATOES AND SHELLFISH

COLOURFUL AND DELICIOUS, THIS TYPICAL GENOESE DISH IS IDEAL FOR A DINNER PARTY. THE TOMATO SAUCE IS QUITE RUNNY, SO SERVE IT WITH CRUSTY BREAD AND SPOONS AS WELL AS FORKS.

SERVES FOUR

INGREDIENTS
45ml/3 tbsp olive oil
1 small onion, chopped
1 garlic clove, crushed
½ fresh red chilli, seeded
  and chopped
200g/7oz can chopped
  plum tomatoes
30ml/2 tbsp chopped fresh flat
  leaf parsley
400g/14oz fresh clams
400g/14oz fresh mussels
60ml/4 tbsp dry white wine
400g/14oz/3½ cups dried trenette
  or spaghetti
a few fresh basil leaves
90g/3½oz/⅔ cup cooked, peeled
  prawns (shrimp), thawed and
  thoroughly dried if frozen
salt and ground black pepper
lemon wedges and chopped
  fresh herbs, such as parsley or
  thyme, to garnish

1 Heat 30ml/2tbsp of the oil in a frying pan or medium pan. Add the onion, garlic and chilli and cook over a medium heat for 1–2 minutes, stirring constantly. Stir in the tomatoes, half the parsley and pepper to taste. Bring to the boil, lower the heal, cover and simmer for 15 minutes.

2 Meanwhile, scrub the clams and mussels under cold running water. Discard any that are open and that do not close when sharply tapped against the work surface.

3 In a large pan, heat the remaining oil. Add the clams and mussels, with the rest of the parsley and toss over a high heat for a few seconds. Pour in the wine, then cover tightly. Cook for about 5 minutes, shaking the pan frequently, until the clams and mussels have opened.

4 Transfer the clams and mussels to a bowl, discarding any shellfish that have failed to open. Strain the cooking liquid and set aside. Reserve eight clams and four mussels for the garnish, then remove the rest from their shells.

5 Cook the pasta according to the instructions on the packet. Meanwhile, add 120ml/4fl oz/ ½ cup of the reserved shellfish liquid to the tomato sauce. Add the basil, prawns, shelled clams and mussels to the sauce. Season.

6 Drain the pasta and tip it into a warmed bowl. Add the sauce and toss well to combine. Serve in individual bowls. Sprinkle with herbs and garnish each portion with lemon, two clams and one mussel in their shells.

Per portion: Energy 510Kcal/2160kJ; Protein 27.2g; Carbohydrate 77.1g, of which sugars 5.6g; Fat 11.5g, of which saturates 1.6g; Cholesterol 68mg; Calcium 180mg; Fibre 3.5g; Sodium 193mg.

POTATO GNOCCHI

GNOCCHI CAN BE MADE EITHER WITH MASHED POTATO AND FLOUR, OR WITH SEMOLINA. TO MAKE SURE THAT THEY ARE LIGHT AND FLUFFY, TAKE CARE NOT TO OVERMIX THE DOUGH.

4 Divide the dough into four pieces. On a lightly floured surface, form each into a roll about 2cm/¾in in diameter. Cut the rolls crossways into pieces about 2cm/¾in long.

SERVES FOUR TO SIX

INGREDIENTS
1kg/2¼lb waxy potatoes
250–300g/9–11oz/2¼–2¾ cups
  plain flour (all-purpose), plus more
  if necessary
1 egg
pinch of freshly grated nutmeg
25g/1oz/2 tbsp butter
salt
fresh basil leaves, to garnish
Parmesan cheese cut in shavings,
  to garnish

COOK'S TIP
Gnocchi are also excellent served with a heated sauce, such as Bolognese or a simple cheese sauce.

1 Cook the potatoes in their skins in a large pan of lightly salted, boiling water until tender but not falling apart. Drain and peel while the potatoes are still hot.

2 Spread a layer of flour on a work surface. Pass the hot potatoes through a food mill, dropping them directly on to the flour. Sprinkle with about half of the remaining flour and mix in very lightly. Break the egg into the mixture.

3 Finally, add the nutmeg to the dough and knead lightly, adding more flour if the mixture is too loose. When the dough is light to the touch and no longer moist, it is ready to be rolled.

5 Hold an ordinary table fork with tines sideways, leaning on the board. Then one by one, press and roll the gnocchi lightly along the tines of the fork towards the points, making ridges on one side, and a depression from your thumb on the other.

6 Bring a large pan of salted water to a fast boil, then drop in about half the prepared gnocchi.

7 When the gnocchi rise to the surface, after 3–4 minutes, they are done. Lift them out with a slotted spoon, drain well, and place in a warmed serving bowl. Dot with butter. Cover to keep warm while cooking the remainder. As soon as they are cooked, toss the gnocchi with the butter, garnish with Parmesan shavings and fresh basil leaves, and serve immediately.

Per portion: Energy 454Kcal/1921kJ; Protein 11.7g; Carbohydrate 88.9g, of which sugars 4.2g; Fat 8.1g, of which saturates 4g; Cholesterol 61mg; Calcium 111mg; Fibre 4.5g; Sodium 85mg.

TURKEY LASAGNE

THIS EASY MEAL-IN-ONE BAKED PASTA DISH IS DELICIOUS MADE WITH COOKED TURKEY PIECES AND BROCCOLI IN A RICH, CREAMY PARMESAN SAUCE.

SERVES FOUR

INGREDIENTS
30ml/2 tbsp light olive oil
1 onion, chopped
2 garlic cloves, chopped
450g/1lb cooked turkey meat,
  finely diced
225g/8oz/1 cup mascarpone cheese
30ml/2 tbsp chopped fresh tarragon
300g/11oz broccoli, broken
  into florets
salt and ground black pepper
For the sauce
50g/2oz/¼ cup butter
30ml/2 tbsp plain (all-purpose) flour
600ml/1 pint/2½ cups milk
75g/3oz/1 cup freshly grated
  Parmesan cheese
115g/4oz no pre-cook lasagne verdi

3 To make the sauce, melt the butter in a pan, stir in the flour and cook for 1 minute, still stirring. Remove from the heat and gradually stir in the milk. Return to the heat and bring the sauce to the boil, stirring constantly. Simmer for 1 minute, then add 50g/2oz/⅔ cup of the Parmesan and plenty of salt and pepper.

4 Spoon a layer of the turkey mixture into a large, shallow ovenproof dish. Add a layer of broccoli and cover with sheets of lasagne. Coat with cheese sauce. Repeat these layers, finishing with a layer of cheese sauce on top. Sprinkle with the remaining Parmesan and bake for 35–40 minutes.

1 Preheat the oven to 180°C/350°F/ Gas 4. Heat the oil in a heavy pan and cook the onion and garlic until softened but not coloured. Remove the pan from the heat and stir in the diced turkey, mascarpone and tarragon and season with salt and pepper to taste.

2 Blanch the broccoli in a large pan of salted, boiling water for 1 minute, then drain and rinse thoroughly under cold water to prevent the broccoli from overcooking. Drain well and set aside.

COOK'S TIP
This is a delicious way of using up any cooked turkey that is left over after Christmas or Thanksgiving celebrations. It is also especially good made with half ham and half turkey.

Per portion: Energy 732Kcal/3072kJ; Protein 61.6g; Carbohydrate 43g, of which sugars 13.1g; Fat 36.2g, of which saturates 19.4g; Cholesterol 138mg; Calcium 539mg; Fibre 3.6g; Sodium 475mg.

SEAFOOD LASAGNE

THIS DISH CAN BE AS SIMPLE OR AS ELEGANT AS YOU LIKE. FOR A DINNER PARTY, DRESS IT UP WITH SCALLOPS, MUSSELS OR PRAWNS AND A REALLY GENEROUS PINCH OF SAFFRON IN THE SAUCE; FOR A FAMILY SUPPER, USE SIMPLE FISH, SUCH AS COD AND SMOKED HADDOCK. THE LASAGNE CAN BE PREPARED IN ADVANCE AND BAKED AT THE LAST MOMENT.

SERVES EIGHT

INGREDIENTS
    350g/12oz monkfish
    350g/12oz salmon fillet
    350g/12oz undyed smoked haddock
    1 litre/1¾ pints/4 cups milk
    500ml/17fl oz/generous 2 cups
        fish stock
    2 bay leaves or a good pinch of
        saffron threads
    1 small onion, peeled and halved
    75g/3oz/6 tbsp butter, plus extra
        for greasing
    45ml/3 tbsp plain (all-purpose) flour
    150g/5oz/2 cups mushrooms, sliced
    225–300g/8–11oz no-precook or
        fresh lasagne
    60ml/4 tbsp freshly grated
        Parmesan cheese
    salt, ground black pepper, grated
        nutmeg and paprika
    rocket (arugula) leaves, to garnish
For the tomato sauce
    30ml/2 tbsp olive oil
    1 red onion, finely chopped
    1 garlic clove, finely chopped
    400g/14oz can chopped tomatoes
    15ml/1 tbsp tomato purée (paste)
    15ml/1 tbsp torn fresh basil leaves

1 Make the tomato sauce. Heat the oil in a pan and cook the onion and garlic over a low heat for 5 minutes, until softened and golden. Stir in the tomatoes and tomato purée and simmer for 20–30 minutes, stirring occasionally. Season to taste with salt and pepper and stir in the basil.

COOK'S TIP
It is preferable to use fresh lasagne, if available, as it has a better flavour and texture. Cook the sheets, in batches if necessary, in a large pan of lightly salted, boiling water for 3 minutes. Do not overcrowd the pan or the sheets will stick together.

2 Put all the fish in a shallow flameproof dish or pan with the milk, stock, bay leaves or saffron and onion. Bring to the boil over a medium heat. Poach for 5 minutes, until almost cooked. Leave to cool.

3 When the fish is almost cold, strain it, reserving the liquid. Remove the skin and any bones and flake the flesh.

4 Preheat the oven to 180°C/350°F/ Gas 4. Melt the butter in a pan, stir in the flour; cook for 2 minutes, stirring. Gradually add the poaching liquid and bring to the boil, stirring. Add the mushrooms, cook for 2–3 minutes; season with salt, pepper and nutmeg.

5 Lightly grease a shallow ovenproof dish. Spoon a thin layer of the mushroom sauce over the base of the dish and spread it with a spatula. Stir the fish into the remaining mushroom sauce in the pan.

6 Make a layer of lasagne, then a layer of fish and sauce. Add another layer of lasagne, then spread over all the tomato sauce. Continue to layer the lasagne and fish, finish with a layer of lasagne.

7 Sprinkle over the grated Parmesan cheese. Bake for 30–45 minutes, until bubbling and golden. Before serving, sprinkle with paprika and garnish with rocket leaves.

Per portion: Energy 411Kcal/1724kJ; Protein 32.2g; Carbohydrate 29.8g, of which sugars 3.6g; Fat 18.9g, of which saturates 7.8g; Cholesterol 71mg; Calcium 143mg; Fibre 1.9g; Sodium 525mg.

SICHUAN NOODLES WITH SESAME SAUCE

THIS CHINESE VEGETARIAN DISH RESEMBLES THAMIN LETHOK, A BURMESE DISH, WHICH CONSISTS OF FLAVOURED NOODLES SERVED WITH SEPARATE VEGETABLES THAT ARE TOSSED AT THE TABLE.

SERVES THREE TO FOUR

INGREDIENTS

450g/1lb fresh or 225g/8oz dried
   egg noodles
1/2 cucumber, sliced lengthways,
   seeded and diced
4–6 spring onions (scallions)
a bunch of radishes, about 115g/4oz
225g/8oz mooli (daikon), peeled
115g/4oz/2 cups beansprouts, rinsed
   then left in iced water and drained
60ml/4 tbsp groundnut (peanut) oil
   or sunflower oil
2 garlic cloves, crushed
45ml/3 tbsp toasted sesame paste
15ml/1 tbsp sesame oil
15ml/1 tbsp light soy sauce
5–10ml/1–2 tsp chilli sauce, to taste
15ml/1 tbsp rice vinegar
120ml/4fl oz/1/2 cup chicken stock
   or water
5ml/1 tsp sugar, or to taste
salt and ground black pepper
roasted peanuts or cashew nuts

1 If using fresh noodles, cook them in boiling water for 1 minute, then drain well. Rinse the noodles in cold fresh water and drain again. If using dry noodles, cook the dried noodles according to the instructions on the packet, draining and rinsing them as you would for fresh noodles.

2 Sprinkle the cucumber with salt, leave for 15 minutes, rinse well, then drain and pat dry on kitchen paper. Place in a large salad bowl.

3 Cut the spring onions into fine shreds. Cut the radishes in half and slice finely. Coarsely grate the mooli using a mandolin or a food processor. Add all the vegetables to the cucumber and toss gently.

4 Heat half the oil in a wok or frying pan and stir-fry the noodles for about 1 minute. Using a slotted spoon, transfer the noodles to a large serving bowl and keep warm.

5 Add the remaining oil to the wok. When it is hot, cook the garlic to flavour the oil. Remove from the heat and stir in the sesame paste, with the sesame oil, soy and chilli sauces, vinegar and stock or water. Add a little sugar and season to taste. Warm through over a gentle heat. Do not overheat or the sauce will thicken too much. Pour the sauce over the noodles and toss well. Garnish with peanuts or cashew nuts and serve with the vegetables.

Per portion: Energy 383Kcal/1592kJ; Protein 8.7g; Carbohydrate 24.9g, of which sugars 4.8g; Fat 28.3g, of which saturates 3.9g; Cholesterol 9mg; Calcium 153mg; Fibre 4.2g; Sodium 398mg.

RICE NOODLES WITH PORK

ALTHOUGH RICE NOODLES HAVE LITTLE FLAVOUR THEMSELVES, THEY HAVE A WONDERFUL ABILITY TO TAKE ON THE FLAVOUR OF OTHER INGREDIENTS.

SERVES FOUR TO SIX

INGREDIENTS
   450g/1lb pork fillet (tenderloin)
   225g/8oz dried rice noodles
   115g/4oz/1 cup broccoli florets
   1 red (bell) pepper, quartered
      and seeded
   45ml/3 tbsp groundnut (peanut) oil
   2 garlic cloves, crushed
   10 spring onions (scallions), cut into
      5cm/2in diagonal slices
   1 lemon grass stalk, finely chopped
   1–2 fresh red chillies, seeded and
      finely chopped
   300ml/½ pint/1¼ cups coconut milk
   15ml/1 tbsp tomato purée (paste)
   3 kaffir lime leaves (optional)
For the marinade
   45ml/3 tbsp light soy sauce
   15ml/1 tbsp rice wine
   30ml/2 tbsp groundnut (peanut) oil
   2.5cm/1in piece of fresh root ginger

1 Cut the pork into strips 2.5cm/1in long and 1cm/½in wide. Mix all the marinade ingredients in a bowl, add the pork, stir and marinate for 1 hour.

2 Spread out the rice noodles in a large, shallow dish, pour over enough hot water to cover and leave to soak for 20 minutes, until soft. Drain well and set aside.

3 Meanwhile, blanch the broccoli florets in a small pan of boiling water for 2 minutes, then drain, refresh under cold water and drain well again. Set aside until required.

4 Place the pepper pieces under a hot grill (broiler) for a few minutes until the skin blackens and blisters. Put in a plastic bag for about 10 minutes and then, when cool enough to handle, peel off the skin and slice the flesh thinly.

5 Drain the pork, reserving the marinade. Heat 30ml/2 tbsp of the oil in a large frying pan. Stir-fry the pork, in batches if necessary, for about 3–4 minutes, until the meat is tender. Transfer to a plate and keep warm.

6 Add a little more oil to the pan if necessary and stir-fry the garlic, spring onions, lemon grass and chillies over a low to medium heat for 2–3 minutes. Add the broccoli and pepper slices and stir-fry for a few minutes more.

7 Stir in the reserved marinade, coconut milk and tomato purée, with the kaffir lime leaves, if using. Simmer gently until the broccoli is nearly tender, then add the pork and noodles. Toss over the heat for 3–4 minutes until completely heated through. Transfer to a warm dish and serve immediately.

Per portion: Energy 454Kcal/1901kJ; Protein 30.1g; Carbohydrate 53.2g, of which sugars 7.1g; Fat 12.8g, of which saturates 3.2g; Cholesterol 70mg; Calcium 57mg; Fibre 1.5g; Sodium 428mg.

PAN-FRIED
& GRILLED

Some of the most mouthwatering but simplest dishes are grilled, or sizzled on top of the stove. Grilling food is healthier, and there's also something about this way of cooking that makes the food look and taste great. With pan-fried dishes, the texture is often crisp on the outside, but beneath, the food is beautifully tender and moist. In this chapter you will find delights to feast on like Potato and Onion Cakes with Beetroot Relish, and Trout with Tamarind and Chilli Sauce, as well as appetizing pan-fried dishes such as Salt Cod Fritters with Aioli and Lamb Burgers with Red Onion and Tomato Relish.

SALT COD FRITTERS <u>WITH</u> AIOLI

AIOLI IS A FIERCELY GARLICKY, OLIVE OIL MAYONNAISE FROM PROVENCE IN THE SOUTH OF FRANCE AND IS A TRADITIONAL ACCOMPANIMENT TO SALT COD.

SERVES SIX

INGREDIENTS
   450g/1lb salt cod
   500g/1¼lb floury potatoes
   300ml/½ pint/1¼ cups milk
   6 spring onions (scallions),
    finely chopped
   30ml/2 tbsp extra virgin olive oil
   30ml/2 tbsp chopped fresh parsley
   juice of ½ lemon, to taste
   2 eggs, beaten
   60ml/4 tbsp plain (all-purpose) flour
   90g/3½oz/1⅓ cups dry
    white breadcrumbs
   vegetable oil, for shallow frying
   salt and ground black pepper
   lemon wedges and salad, to serve
For the aioli
   2 large garlic cloves
   2 egg yolks
   300ml/½ pint/1¼ cups olive oil
   lemon juice, to taste

1 Soak the salt cod in cold water for 24–36 hours, changing the water 5–6 times. It swells as it rehydrates and a tiny piece should not taste too salty when tried. Drain well.

2 Cook the potatoes, unpeeled, in a pan of boiling salted water for about 20 minutes, until tender. Drain, then peel and mash the potatoes.

3 Poach the cod very gently in the milk with half the spring onions for 10–15 minutes, or until it flakes easily. Remove the cod and flake it with a fork into a bowl, discarding bones and skin.

4 Add 60ml/4 tbsp mashed potato to the flaked cod and beat with a wooden spoon. Work in the olive oil, then gradually add the remaining potato. Beat in the remaining spring onions and the parsley. Season with lemon juice and pepper to taste – the mixture may need a little salt. Beat in one egg, then chill the mixture until firm.

5 Shape the mixture into 12–18 small round cakes. Coat them in flour, then dip them in the remaining egg and coat with the breadcrumbs. Chill.

COOK'S TIPS
• Try to find a thick, creamy white piece of salt cod, preferably cut from the middle of the fish rather than the tail and fin ends. Avoid thin, yellowish salt cod, as it will be too dry and salty.
• Mash potatoes by hand, never in a food processor, as it makes them gluey.
• Aioli traditionally has a sharp bite from the raw garlic. However, if you prefer a milder flavour, blanch the garlic once or twice in boiling water for about 3 minutes each time before using it.

6 Meanwhile, make the aioli. Place the garlic and a good pinch of salt in a mortar and pound to a paste with a pestle. Transfer to a bowl and using a small whisk or a wooden spoon, gradually work in the egg yolks.

7 Add the olive oil, a drop at a time, until half is incorporated. When the sauce is as thick as soft butter, beat in 5–10ml/ 1–2 tsp lemon juice, then continue adding oil until the aioli is very thick. Adjust the seasoning, adding lemon juice to taste.

8 Heat about 2cm/¾in depth of oil in a large, heavy frying pan. Add the salt cod fritters and cook over a medium-high heat for about 4 minutes. Turn them over and cook for a further 4 minutes on the other side, until crisp and golden. Drain on crumpled kitchen paper, then serve with the aioli, lemon wedges and salad leaves.

Per portion: Energy 718Kcal/2980kJ; Protein 21.1g; Carbohydrate 33.1g, of which sugars 1.9g; Fat 56.5g, of which saturates 8.3g; Cholesterol 165mg; Calcium 67mg; Fibre 1.6g; Sodium 196mg.

CHEESE AND LEEK SAUSAGES WITH TOMATO, GARLIC AND CHILLI SAUCE

THIS TRADITIONAL WELSH SPECIALITY IS TRADITIONALLY MADE USING BREADCRUMBS ALONE. ADDING A LITTLE MASHED POTATO, HOWEVER, LIGHTENS THE SAUSAGES AND MAKES THEM EASIER TO HANDLE.

1 Melt the butter and cook the leeks for 4–5 minutes, until softened but not browned. Mix with the mashed potato, fresh breadcrumbs, cheese, parsley and sage or marjoram. Add sufficient beaten egg (about two-thirds of the quantity) to bind the mixture. Season well and add a good pinch of cayenne.

2 Shape the mixture into 12 sausage shapes. Dip in the remaining egg, then coat with the dry breadcrumbs. Chill the coated sausages.

3 To make the sauce, heat the oil over a low heat in a pan, add the garlic, chilli and onion and cook for 3–4 minutes. Add the tomatoes, thyme and vinegar. Season with salt, pepper and sugar.

4 Cook the sauce for 40–50 minutes, until much reduced. Remove the thyme and purée the sauce in a blender. Reheat with the marjoram or oregano, then adjust the seasoning, adding more sugar, if necessary.

5 Cook the sausages in shallow oil until golden brown on all sides. Drain on kitchen paper and serve with the sauce.

COOK'S TIP
These sausages are also delicious served with garlic mayonnaise.

SERVES FOUR

INGREDIENTS
25g/1oz/2 tbsp butter
175g/6oz leeks, finely chopped
90ml/6 tbsp cold mashed potato
115g/4oz/2 cups fresh white or
  wholemeal (whole-wheat)
  breadcrumbs
150g/5oz/1¼ cups grated Caerphilly,
  Lancashire or Cantal cheese
30ml/2 tbsp chopped fresh parsley
5ml/1 tsp chopped fresh sage
  or marjoram
2 large (US extra large) eggs, beaten
cayenne pepper
65g/2½oz/1 cup dry white
  breadcrumbs
oil for shallow frying

For the sauce
30ml/2 tbsp olive oil
2 garlic cloves, thinly sliced
1 fresh red chilli, seeded and finely
  chopped, or a good pinch of dried
  red chilli flakes
1 small onion, finely chopped
500g/1¼lb tomatoes, peeled,
  seeded and chopped
few fresh thyme sprigs
10ml/2 tsp balsamic vinegar or red
  wine vinegar
pinch of light muscovado
  (brown) sugar
15–30ml/1–2 tbsp chopped fresh
  marjoram or oregano
salt and ground black pepper

Per portion: Energy 580Kcal/2416kJ; Protein 19.2g; Carbohydrate 35.5g, of which sugars 7g; Fat 40.3g, of which saturates 15.2g; Cholesterol 164mg; Calcium 361mg; Fibre 3.5g; Sodium 604mg.

POTATO <u>AND</u> ONION CAKES <u>WITH</u> BEETROOT RELISH

THESE IRRESISTIBLE PANCAKES ARE BASED ON TRADITIONAL EASTERN EUROPEAN LATKE, GRATED POTATO CAKES. THEY ARE DELICIOUS WITH A SWEET-SHARP BEETROOT RELISH AND SOUR CREAM.

SERVES FOUR

INGREDIENTS
500g/1¼lb potatoes
1 small cooking apple, peeled, cored
  and coarsely grated
1 small onion, finely chopped
50g/2oz/½ cup plain (all-
  purpose) flour
2 large (US extra large) eggs, beaten
30ml/2 tbsp chopped chives
vegetable oil, for shallow frying
salt and ground black pepper
250ml/8fl oz/1 cup sour cream
  or crème fraîche
fresh dill sprigs and fresh chives
  or chive flowers, to garnish
For the beetroot (beet) relish
250g/9oz beetroot (beet), cooked
  and peeled
1 large eating apple, cored and
  finely diced
15ml/1 tbsp finely chopped red onion
15–30ml/1–2 tbsp tarragon vinegar
15ml/1 tbsp chopped fresh dill
15–30ml/1–2 tbsp light olive oil
pinch of caster (superfine) sugar

1 To make the relish, finely dice the beetroot, then mix it with the apple and onion. Add 15ml/1 tbsp of the vinegar, the dill and 15ml/1 tbsp of the oil. Season, adding more vinegar and oil, and a pinch of caster sugar to taste.

2 Coarsely grate the potatoes, then rinse in cold water, drain and dry them on a clean dishtowel.

3 Mix the potatoes, apple and onion in a bowl. Stir in the flour, eggs and chives. Season and mix again.

4 Heat about 5mm/¼in depth of oil in a frying pan and cook spoonfuls of the mixture. Flatten them to make pancakes 7.5–10cm/3–4in across and cook for 3–4 minutes on each side, until browned. Drain on kitchen paper and keep warm until the mixture is used up.

5 Serve a stack of pancakes – there should be about 16–20 in total – with spoonfuls of sour cream or crème fraîche, and beetroot relish. Garnish with dill sprigs and chives or chive flowers and grind black pepper on top just before serving.

VARIATION
To make a leek and potato cake, melt 25g/1oz/2 tbsp butter in a pan, add 400g/14oz thinly sliced leeks and cook until tender. Season well. Coarsely grate 500g/1¼lb peeled potatoes, then season. Melt another 25g/1oz/2 tbsp butter in a medium frying pan and add a layer of half the potatoes. Cover with the leeks, then add the remaining potatoes, pressing down with a spatula to form a cake. Cook for 20–25 minutes over a low heat until the potatoes are browned, then turn over and cook for 15–20 minutes to brown the other side.

Per portion: Energy 471Kcal/1964kJ; Protein 10.3g; Carbohydrate 42.1g, of which sugars 13.4g; Fat 30.2g, of which saturates 10.6g; Cholesterol 152mg; Calcium 118mg; Fibre 3.7g; Sodium 125mg.

GRILLED AUBERGINE PARCELS

THESE ARE DELICIOUS LITTLE ITALIAN BUNDLES OF PLUM TOMATOES, MOZZARELLA CHEESE AND FRESH BASIL LEAVES, WRAPPED IN SLICES OF AUBERGINE.

SERVES FOUR

INGREDIENTS
    2 large, long aubergines (eggplant)
    225g/8oz mozzarella cheese
    2 plum tomatoes
    16 large fresh basil leaves
    30ml/2 tbsp olive oil
    salt and ground black pepper
For the dressing
    60ml/4 tbsp olive oil
    5ml/1 tsp balsamic vinegar
    15ml/1 tbsp sun-dried tomato paste
    15ml/1 tbsp lemon juice
For the garnish
    30ml/2 tbsp roasted pine nuts
    torn basil leaves

1 Remove and discard the stalks from the aubergines and cut them lengthways into thin slices – the aim is to get 16 slices in total (disregarding the first and last slices), each about 5mm/¼in thick.

2 Bring a large pan of salted water to the boil and cook the aubergine slices for about 2 minutes, until just softened. Drain, then dry on kitchen paper.

3 Cut the mozzarella cheese into eight slices. Cut each tomato into eight slices, not counting the first and last slices.

4 Place two aubergine slices on a baking sheet in a cross. Place a tomato slice in the centre, season, then add a basil leaf, followed by a slice of mozzarella, a basil leaf, a tomato slice and more seasoning.

5 Fold the ends of the aubergine slices around the filling to make a neat parcel. Repeat with the rest of the ingredients to make eight parcels. Chill for about 20 minutes. Preheat the grill (broiler).

6 To make the tomato dressing, whisk all the ingredients together and season to taste.

7 Brush the parcels with the oil and cook for about 5 minutes on each side, until golden. Serve, with the dressing, sprinkled with pine nuts and basil.

Per portion: Energy 370Kcal/1532kJ; Protein 12.9g; Carbohydrate 4.4g, of which sugars 4.2g; Fat 33.6g, of which saturates 10.6g; Cholesterol 33mg; Calcium 219mg; Fibre 2.7g; Sodium 237mg.

GRILLED POLENTA WITH TALEGGIO CHEESE

SLICES OF GRILLED POLENTA, ONE OF THE STAPLES OF NORTH ITALIAN COOKING, ARE TASTY TOPPED WITH SLOWLY CARAMELIZED ONIONS AND BUBBLING TALEGGIO, ALSO FROM NORTH ITALY.

SERVES FOUR

INGREDIENTS
900ml/1½ pints/3¾ cups water
5ml/1 tsp salt
150g/5oz/generous 1 cup polenta
  or cornmeal
50g/2oz/⅓ cup freshly grated
  Parmesan cheese
5ml/1 tsp chopped fresh thyme
90ml/6 tbsp olive oil
675g/1½lb onions, halved
  and sliced
2 garlic cloves, chopped
a few fresh thyme sprigs
5ml/1 tsp brown sugar
15–30ml/1–2 tbsp balsamic vinegar
2 heads radicchio, cut into thick
  slices or wedges
225g/8oz Taleggio cheese, sliced
salt and ground black pepper

1 In a large pan, bring the water to the boil and add the salt. Adjust the heat so that it simmers. Stirring constantly, add the polenta in a steady stream, then bring to the boil. Cook over a very low heat, stirring frequently, for about 30–40 minutes, until thick and smooth.

2 Beat in the Parmesan and chopped thyme, then turn on to a work surface or tray. Spread evenly, then leave to cool.

3 Heat 30ml/2 tbsp of the oil in a frying pan over a moderate heat. Add the onions and stir to coat in the oil, then cover and cook over a very low heat for 15 minutes, stirring occasionally.

4 Add the garlic and most of the thyme sprigs and cook, uncovered, for another 10 minutes, or until light brown.

5 Add the sugar, 15ml/1 tbsp of the vinegar and salt and pepper. Cook for another 5–10 minutes, until soft and well-browned. Taste and add more vinegar and seasoning as necessary.

6 Preheat the grill (broiler). Cut the polenta into thick slices and brush with a little of the remaining oil, then grill (broil) until crusty and lightly browned.

7 Turn over the polenta and add the radicchio to the grill rack or pan. Season the radicchio and brush with a little oil. Grill for about 5 minutes, until the polenta and radicchio are browned. Drizzle a little vinegar over the radicchio.

8 Heap the onions on to the polenta. Sprinkle the cheese and a few sprigs of thyme over both polenta and radicchio. Grill until the cheese is bubbling. Season with pepper and serve immediately.

Per portion: Energy 608Kcal/2522kJ; Protein 22.3g; Carbohydrate 42.7g, of which sugars 11.4g; Fat 37.5g, of which saturates 15.2g; Cholesterol 65mg; Calcium 352mg; Fibre 3.7g; Sodium 456mg.

FRIED FISH WITH TOMATO SAUCE

This simple dish is perennially popular with children. It works equally well with lemon sole or dabs (these do not need skinning), or fillets of haddock and whiting.

SERVES FOUR

INGREDIENTS

60ml/4 tbsp plain (all-purpose) flour
2 eggs, beaten
75g/3oz/¾ cup dried breadcrumbs
4 small plaice or flounder, dark
  skin removed
15g/½oz/1 tbsp butter
15ml/1 tbsp sunflower oil
salt and ground black pepper
1 lemon, quartered, to serve
fresh basil leaves, to garnish
For the tomato sauce
30ml/2 tbsp olive oil
1 red onion, finely chopped
1 garlic clove, finely chopped
400g/14oz can chopped tomatoes
15ml/1 tbsp tomato purée (paste)
15ml/1 tbsp torn fresh basil leaves

1 First make the tomato sauce. Heat the olive oil in a large pan, add the finely chopped onion and garlic and cook gently for about 5 minutes, until softened and pale golden. Stir in the chopped tomatoes and tomato purée and simmer for 20–30 minutes, stirring occasionally. Season with salt and pepper and stir in the basil.

2 Spread out the flour in a shallow dish, pour the beaten eggs into another and spread out the breadcrumbs in a third. Season the fish with salt and pepper.

3 Hold a fish in your left hand and dip it first in flour, then in egg and finally in the breadcrumbs, patting the crumbs on with your dry right hand.

4 Heat the butter and oil in a frying pan until foaming. Cook the fish, one at a time, in the hot fat for about 5 minutes on each side, until golden brown and cooked through, but still juicy in the middle. Drain on kitchen paper and keep hot while you cook the rest. Serve with lemon wedges and the tomato sauce, garnished with basil leaves.

Per portion: Energy 345Kcal/1445kJ; Protein 23g; Carbohydrate 28.3g, of which sugars 5.6g; Fat 16.3g, of which saturates 4.2g; Cholesterol 144mg; Calcium 105mg; Fibre 2g; Sodium 338mg.

TROUT WITH TAMARIND AND CHILLI SAUCE

ALTHOUGH VERY ECONOMICAL, TROUT CAN TASTE RATHER BLAND. THIS SPICY THAI-INSPIRED SAUCE REALLY GIVES IT ZING. IF YOU LIKE YOUR FOOD VERY SPICY, ADD AN EXTRA CHILLI.

SERVES FOUR

INGREDIENTS
    4 trout, 350g/12oz each, cleaned
    6 spring onions (scallions), sliced
    60ml/4 tbsp soy sauce
    15ml/1 tbsp stir-fry oil
    30ml/2 tbsp chopped fresh
        coriander (cilantro)
For the sauce
    50g/2oz tamarind pulp
    105ml/7 tbsp boiling water
    2 shallots, coarsely chopped
    1 fresh red chilli, seeded
        and chopped
    1cm/½in piece fresh root ginger,
        peeled and chopped
    5ml/1 tsp soft brown sugar
    45ml/3 tbsp Thai fish sauce

1 Slash the trout diagonally four or five times on each side with a sharp knife and place in a shallow dish.

2 Fill the cavities with spring onions and douse each fish with soy sauce. Carefully turn the fish over to coat both sides with the sauce. Sprinkle on any remaining spring onions and set aside until required.

3 Make the sauce. Put the tamarind pulp in a small bowl and pour on the boiling water. Mash well with a fork until soft. Tip the mixture into a food processor or blender, add the shallots, fresh chilli, chopped ginger, brown sugar and Thai fish sauce and process to a coarse pulp.

4 Heat the stir-fry oil in a large frying pan or wok and cook the trout, one at a time if necessary, for about 5 minutes on each side, until the skin is crisp and browned and the flesh cooked. Put on warmed plates and spoon over some sauce. Sprinkle with the coriander and serve with the remaining sauce.

Per portion: Energy 352Kcal/1481kJ; Protein 55g; Carbohydrate 3.3g, of which sugars 2.8g; Fat 13.4g, of which saturates 2.8g; Cholesterol 224mg; Calcium 95mg; Fibre 0.4g; Sodium 721mg.

SEARED TUNA STEAKS WITH ONION SALSA

RED ONIONS ARE IDEAL FOR THIS SALSA, NOT ONLY FOR THEIR MILD AND SWEET FLAVOUR, BUT ALSO BECAUSE THEY LOOK SO APPETIZING. SALAD, RICE OR BREAD AND A BOWL OF THICK YOGURT FLAVOURED WITH CHOPPED FRESH HERBS ARE GOOD ACCOMPANIMENTS.

1 Wash the tuna steaks and pat dry. Sprinkle with half the cumin, the dried chilli, salt, pepper and half the lime rind. Rub in 30ml/2 tbsp of the oil and set aside in a glass or china dish for about 30 minutes.

2 Meanwhile, make the salsa. Mix the onion, tomatoes, avocado, kiwi fruit, fresh chilli, chopped coriander and mint. Add the remaining cumin, the rest of the lime rind and half the lime juice. Season with Thai fish sauce and sugar to taste. Set aside for 15–20 minutes, then add more Thai fish sauce, lime juice and olive oil if required.

3 Heat a ridged, cast–iron griddle pan. Cook the tuna, allowing about 2 minutes on each side for rare tuna or a little longer for a medium result.

4 Serve the tuna steaks garnished with lime wedges and coriander sprigs. Serve the salsa separately or spoon on to the plates with the tuna.

SERVES FOUR

INGREDIENTS
    4 tuna steaks, each weighing about
        175–200g/6–7oz
    5ml/1 tsp cumin seeds, toasted
        and crushed
    pinch of dried red chilli flakes
    grated rind and juice of 1 lime
    30–60ml/2–4 tbsp extra virgin
        olive oil
    salt and ground black pepper
    lime wedges and fresh coriander
        (cilantro) sprigs, to garnish

For the salsa
    1 small red onion, finely chopped
    200g/7oz red or yellow cherry
        tomatoes, coarsely chopped
    1 avocado, peeled, stoned
        (pitted) and chopped
    2 kiwi fruit, peeled and chopped
    1 fresh red chilli, seeded and
        finely chopped
    15g/½oz fresh coriander
        (cilantro), chopped
    6 fresh mint sprigs, leaves
        only, chopped
    5–10ml/1–2 tsp Thai fish sauce
    about 5ml/1 tsp muscovado
        (molasses) sugar

Per portion: Energy 389Kcal/1628kJ; Protein 43.2g; Carbohydrate 7.9g, of which sugars 6.8g; Fat 20.7g, of which saturates 4.4g; Cholesterol 49mg; Calcium 55mg; Fibre 2.5g; Sodium 180mg.

ROMANIAN KEBABS

KEBABS ARE POPULAR WORLDWIDE, LARGELY BECAUSE THEY ARE SO EASILY ADAPTED TO SUIT EVERYONE'S TASTE. IN THIS RECIPE, LEAN LAMB IS MARINATED, THEN COOKED WITH CHUNKS OF VEGETABLES TO PRODUCE A DELICIOUS, COLOURFUL AND HEALTHY MEAL.

SERVES SIX

INGREDIENTS
675g/1½lb lean lamb, cut into
    4cm/1½in cubes
12 button (pearl) onions
2 green (bell) peppers, seeded and
    cut into 12 pieces
12 cherry tomatoes
12 button (white) mushrooms
lemon slices and fresh rosemary
    sprigs, to garnish
freshly cooked rice and crusty bread,
    to serve
For the marinade
    juice of 1 lemon
    120ml/4fl oz/½ cup red wine
    1 onion, finely chopped
    60ml/4 tbsp olive oil
    2.5ml/½ tsp dried sage
    2.5ml/½ tsp chopped fresh rosemary
    salt and ground black pepper

VARIATIONS
• Use rump (round) steak instead of lamb. Cut it into strips, marinate it as suggested, then interleave the strips on the skewers, with the onions, cherry tomatoes and mushrooms. Omit the green (bell) peppers.
• These kebabs are just as delicious cooked on a barbecue.

1 For the marinade, combine the lemon juice, red wine, onion, olive oil, herbs and seasoning in a bowl. Stir the cubes of lamb into the marinade. Cover and chill in the refrigerator for 2–12 hours, stirring occasionally.

2 Remove the lamb pieces from the marinade and thread on six skewers with the onions, peppers, tomatoes and mushrooms. Preheat the grill (broiler).

3 Brush the kebabs with marinade and grill (broil) for 10–15 minutes, turning once. Arrange on cooked rice, with lemon and rosemary. Serve with crusty bread.

Per portion: Energy 259Kcal/1083kJ; Protein 23.6g; Carbohydrate 4g, of which sugars 3.4g; Fat 16.7g, of which saturates 6.5g; Cholesterol 86mg; Calcium 22mg; Fibre 1.9g; Sodium 104mg.

JERUSALEM BARBECUE LAMB KEBABS

This Israeli dish is traditionally made with turkey and a little lamb fat, or with chicken and a small amount of veal. Turkey, chicken, beef and veal can all be cooked in this way.

SERVES FOUR TO SIX

INGREDIENTS

   800g/1¾lb tender lamb, cubed
   1.5ml/¼ tsp ground allspice
   1.5ml/¼ tsp ground cinnamon
   1.5ml/¼ tsp ground black pepper
   1.5ml/¼ tsp ground cardamom
   45–60ml/3–4 tbsp chopped
     fresh parsley
   2 onions, chopped
   5–8 garlic cloves, chopped
   juice of ½ lemon or 45ml/3 tbsp dry
     white wine
   45ml/3 tbsp extra virgin olive oil
   sumac, for sprinkling (optional)
   30ml/2 tbsp pine nuts
   salt
For serving
   flat breads, such as pitta bread,
     tortillas or naan bread
   tahini
   crunchy vegetable salad

1 Put the lamb, allspice, cinnamon, black pepper, cardamom, half the parsley, half the onions, the garlic, lemon juice or wine and olive oil in a bowl and mix together. Season with salt now, if you like, or sprinkle on after cooking. Set aside and leave to marinate.

COOK'S TIPS

• These kebabs can also be cooked under a hot grill (broiler).

2 Meanwhile, light the barbecue and leave for about 40 minutes. When the coals are white and grey, the barbecue is ready for cooking. If using wooden skewers, soak them in water for about 30 minutes to prevent them from burning.

3 Thread the cubes of meat on to wooden or metal skewers, then cook on the barbecue for 2–3 minutes on each side, turning occasionally, until cooked evenly and browned.

4 Transfer the kebabs to a serving dish and sprinkle with the reserved onions, parsley, sumac, if using, pine nuts and salt, if you like. Serve the kebabs with warmed flat breads to wrap the kebabs in, a bowl of tahini for drizzling over and a vegetable salad.

Per portion: Energy 513Kcal/2137kJ; Protein 41.4g; Carbohydrate 6.4g, of which sugars 4.7g; Fat 36g, of which saturates 11.9g; Cholesterol 152mg; Calcium 51mg; Fibre 1.6g; Sodium 177mg.

LAMB BURGERS WITH RELISH

A SHARP-SWEET RED ONION RELISH WORKS WELL WITH BURGERS BASED ON MIDDLE-EASTERN STYLE LAMB. SERVE WITH PITTA BREAD AND TABBOULEH OR WITH FRIES AND A CRISP GREEN SALAD.

SERVES FOUR

INGREDIENTS
  25g/1oz/3 tbsp bulgur wheat
  500g/1¼lb lean minced
    (ground) lamb
  1 small red onion, finely chopped
  2 garlic cloves, finely chopped
  1 green chilli, seeded and
    finely chopped
  5ml/1 tsp ground toasted cumin seeds
  2.5ml/½ tsp ground sumac
  15g/½oz chopped fresh flat
    leaf parsley
  30ml/2 tbsp chopped fresh mint
  olive oil, for frying
  salt and ground black pepper
For the relish
  2 red (bell) peppers, halved
    and seeded
  2 red onions, cut into 5mm/¼in
    thick slices
  75–90ml/5–6 tbsp extra virgin olive oil
  350g/12oz cherry tomatoes, chopped
  ½–1 fresh red or green chilli, seeded
    and finely chopped (optional)
  30ml/2 tbsp chopped fresh mint
  30ml/2 tbsp chopped fresh parsley
  15ml/1 tbsp chopped fresh oregano
  2.5–5ml/½–1 tsp each ground toasted
    cumin seeds
  2.5–5ml/½–1 tsp sumac
  juice of ½ lemon
  caster (superfine) sugar, to taste

1 Pour 150ml/¼ pint/⅔ cup hot water over the bulgur wheat in a bowl and leave to stand for 15 minutes, then drain in a sieve and squeeze out the excess moisture.

2 Place the bulgur wheat in a bowl and add the minced lamb, onion, garlic, chilli, cumin, sumac, parsley and mint. Mix the ingredients thoroughly together by hand, then season with 5ml/1 tsp salt and plenty of black pepper and mix again. Form the mixture into eight small burgers and set aside in the refrigerator while you make the relish.

3 Grill (broil) the peppers, skin side up, until the skin chars and blisters. Place in a bowl, cover and leave to stand for 10 minutes. Peel off the skin, dice the peppers finely and place in a bowl.

4 Brush the onions with 15ml/1 tbsp oil and grill for 5 minutes on each side, until browned. Cool, then chop.

5 Add the onions, tomatoes, chilli to taste, the mint, parsley, oregano and 2.5ml/½ tsp each of the cumin and sumac to the peppers. Stir in 60ml/4 tbsp of the remaining oil and 15ml/1 tbsp of the lemon juice. Season with salt, pepper and sugar and leave to stand for 20–30 minutes.

6 Heat a heavy frying pan or a ridged, cast-iron griddle pan over a high heat and grease lightly with olive oil. Cook the burgers for about 5–6 minutes on each side, until cooked at the centre.

7 While the burgers are cooking, taste the relish and adjust the seasoning, adding more salt, pepper, sugar, oil, chilli, cumin, sumac and lemon juice to taste. Serve the burgers as soon as they are cooked, with the relish.

Per portion: Energy 537Kcal/2228kJ; Protein 27.2g; Carbohydrate 19g, of which sugars 13.4g; Fat 39.6g, of which saturates 11.1g; Cholesterol 96mg; Calcium 83mg; Fibre 4.2g; Sodium 105mg.

PORK CHOPS <u>WITH</u> CHILLI SALSA

THIN CHOPS OR LOIN STEAKS ARE DELICIOUSLY TENDER AND COOK VERY QUICKLY, SO THIS TASTY DISH IS IDEAL FOR A MIDWEEK FAMILY SUPPER.

SERVES FOUR

INGREDIENTS

   30ml/2 tbsp vegetable oil
   15ml/1 tbsp fresh lemon juice
   10ml/2 tsp ground cumin
   5ml/1 tsp dried oregano
   8 pork loin chops, about
     5mm/¼ in thick
   salt and ground black pepper
For the salsa
   2 fresh hot green chillies
   2 green (bell) peppers, seeded
    and chopped
   1 tomato, peeled and seeded
   ½ onion, coarsely chopped
   4 spring onions (scallions)
   1 pickled jalapeño chilli
   30ml/2 tbsp olive oil
   30ml/2 tbsp fresh lime juice
   45ml/3 tbsp cider vinegar
   5ml/1 tsp salt

1 In a small bowl, combine the vegetable oil, lemon juice, cumin and oregano. Add pepper to taste and stir to mix well.

2 Arrange the pork chops in one layer in a shallow dish. Brush each of them with the oil mixture on both sides. Cover them with clear film (plastic wrap) and set aside to marinate for 2–3 hours or in the refrigerator overnight.

3 For the salsa, roast the chillies over a gas flame, holding them with tongs, until charred on all sides. Alternatively, char the skins under the grill (broiler). Leave to cool for 5 minutes. Wearing rubber gloves, remove the skin. For a less hot flavour, discard the seeds.

4 Place the chillies in a food processor or blender. Add the remaining salsa ingredients. Process until finely chopped but do not purée.

5 Transfer the salsa to a small, heavy pan and simmer 15 minutes, stirring occasionally. Set aside.

6 Season the pork chops to taste with salt and pepper. Heat a ridged griddle pan. Alternatively, preheat the grill (broiler). When hot, add the pork chops and cook for about 5 minutes, until browned on the undersides. Turn and continue cooking for a further 5–7 minutes, until done. Work in batches, if necessary.

7 Serve immediately, with the sour green chilli salsa.

Per portion: Energy 341Kcal/1427kJ; Protein 38.9g; Carbohydrate 5.2g, of which sugars 4.7g; Fat 18.5g, of which saturates 4g; Cholesterol 110mg; Calcium 30mg; Fibre 2.2g; Sodium 623mg.

PORK CHOPS WITH CHILLI-NECTARINE RELISH

A FRUITY SALSA MAKES AN INTERESTING AND TASTY CHANGE FROM THE MORE USUAL APPLE SAUCE. SERVE WITH A FRESH, LEAFY GREEN SALAD AND NECTERINE SLICES.

SERVES FOUR

INGREDIENTS
   250ml/8fl oz/1 cup fresh
      orange juice
   45ml/3 tbsp olive oil
   2 garlic cloves, ground
   5ml/1 tsp ground cumin
   15ml/1 tbsp coarsely ground
      black pepper
   8 pork loin chops, about 2cm/¾in
      thick, well trimmed
   salt
For the relish
   1 small fresh green chilli
   2 nectarines
   30ml/2 tbsp clear honey
   juice of ½ lemon
   250ml/8fl oz/1 cup chicken stock
   1 garlic clove, finely chopped
   ½ onion, finely chopped
   5ml/1 tsp grated fresh root ginger
   1.5ml/¼ tsp salt
   15ml/1 tbsp chopped fresh
      coriander (cilantro)

1 For the relish, roast the chilli over a gas flame, holding it with tongs, until charred on all sides. Alternatively, char the skin under the grill (broiler). Leave to cool for 5 minutes.

2 Wearing rubber gloves, carefully remove the charred skin of the chilli. Discard the seeds if you like a less hot flavour. Finely chop the chilli and place in a heavy pan. Halve the nectarines and remove and discard the stones (pits). Chop the flesh and add to the pan with the chilli.

3 Add the honey, lemon juice, chicken stock, garlic, onion, ginger and salt. Bring to the boil, then simmer, stirring occasionally, for about 30 minutes. Stir in the coriander and set aside.

4 In a small bowl, combine the orange juice, oil, garlic, cumin and pepper. Stir to mix well.

5 Arrange the pork chops, in a single layer, in a shallow, non-metallic dish. Pour over the orange juice mixture and turn to coat. Cover with clear film (plastic wrap) and leave in a cool place to marinate for at least 1 hour or in the refrigerator overnight.

6 Remove the pork chops from the marinade and pat dry with kitchen paper. Season lightly with salt.

7 Heat a ridged griddle pan. When hot, add the pork chops and cook for about 5 minutes, until the undersides are browned. Turn and cook on the other side for a further 10 minutes, until browned. Work in batches if necessary. Serve the chops immediately, with the chilli-nectarine relish.

Per portion: Energy 315Kcal/1321kJ; Protein 43.4g; Carbohydrate 11.4g, of which sugars 11g; Fat 10.9g, of which saturates 3.2g; Cholesterol 126mg; Calcium 28mg; Fibre 0.6g; Sodium 144mg.

PORK AND LEEK SAUSAGES WITH POTATO

LONG, SLOW COOKING IS THE TRICK TO REMEMBER FOR GOOD ONION GRAVY AS THIS REDUCES AND CARAMELIZES THE ONIONS TO CREATE A WONDERFULLY SWEET FLAVOUR. DO NOT BE ALARMED AT THE NUMBER OF ONIONS — THEY REDUCE DRAMATICALLY IN VOLUME DURING COOKING.

2 Remove the pan from the heat and stir in the flour, then gradually stir in the stock. Return the pan to the heat. Bring to the boil, stirring, then simmer for 3 minutes, or until thickened. Season.

3 Meanwhile, cook the potatoes and the pork and leek sausages. First, cook the potatoes in a pan of salted boiling water for 20 minutes, or until tender.

4 Drain the potatoes well and mash them with the butter, whipping cream and wholegrain mustard. Season with salt and pepper to taste.

5 Meanwhile, preheat the grill (broiler) to medium. Arrange the sausages on the grill rack and cook for 15–20 minutes, or until cooked, turning frequently so that they turn an even golden brown all over. Serve the sausages with the creamy mash and plenty of onion gravy.

VARIATION
Pesto and garlic mash is also good with sausages. Instead of the mustard, add 15ml/1 tbsp pesto, 2 crushed garlic cloves and a little olive oil.

SERVES FOUR

INGREDIENTS
  12 pork and leek sausages
  salt and ground black pepper
For the onion gravy
  30ml/2 tbsp olive oil
  25g/1oz/2 tbsp butter
  8 onions, sliced
  5ml/1 tsp caster sugar
  15ml/1 tbsp plain (all-purpose) flour
  300ml/½ pint/1¼ cups beef stock
For the mash
  1.5kg/3¼lb potatoes
  50g/2oz/¼ cup butter
  150ml/¼ pint/⅔ cup whipping cream
  15ml/1 tbsp wholegrain mustard

1 Heat the oil and butter in a large pan until foaming. Add the onions and mix well to coat them in the fat. Cover and cook gently for about 30 minutes, stirring frequently. Add the sugar and cook for a further 5 minutes, or until the onions are softened, reduced and caramelized.

Per portion: Energy 939Kcal/3913kJ; Protein 19.9g; Carbohydrate 85g, of which sugars 16.7g; Fat 60g, of which saturates 28.6g; Cholesterol 133mg; Calcium 179mg; Fibre 6.6g; Sodium 942mg.

FILLET ᴏꜰ BEEF STROGANOFF

*LEGEND HAS IT THAT THIS FAMOUS RUSSIAN RECIPE WAS DEVISED BY COUNT PAUL STROGANOFF'S
COOK TO USE BEEF FROZEN BY THE SIBERIAN CLIMATE. THE STRIPS OF LEAN BEEF WERE SERVED IN A
SOUR CREAM SAUCE FLAVOURED WITH BRANDY.*

SERVES EIGHT

INGREDIENTS
- 1.2kg/2½lb fillet (tenderloin) of beef
- 30ml/2 tbsp plain (all-purpose) flour
- large pinch each of cayenne pepper and paprika
- 75ml/5 tbsp sunflower oil
- 1 large onion, chopped
- 3 garlic cloves, finely chopped
- 450g/1lb/6½ cups chestnut mushrooms, sliced
- 75ml/5 tbsp brandy
- 300ml/½ pint/1¼ cups beef stock or consommé
- 300ml/½ pint/1¼ cups sour cream
- 45ml/3 tbsp chopped fresh flat leaf parsley
- salt and ground black pepper

4 Wipe the pan, then add and heat the remaining oil. Coat a batch of meat with flour, then stir-fry over a high heat until browned. Remove from the pan, then coat and stir-fry another batch. When the last batch of steak is cooked, replace all the meat and vegetables. Add the brandy and simmer until it has almost evaporated.

5 Stir in the stock or consommé and seasoning and cook for 10–15 minutes, stirring frequently, or until the meat is tender and the sauce is thick and glossy. Add the sour cream and sprinkle with chopped parsley. Serve with rice and a simple salad.

1 Thinly slice the fillet of beef across the grain, then cut it into fine strips. Season the flour with the cayenne pepper and paprika.

2 Heat half the oil in a large frying pan, add the onion and garlic and cook gently until the onion has softened.

3 Add the mushrooms and stir-fry over a high heat. Transfer the vegetables and their juices to a dish and set aside.

COOK'S TIP
If you do not have a very large pan, it may be easier to cook the meat and vegetables in two separate pans. A large flameproof casserole may be used.

Per portion: Energy 407Kcal/1693kJ; Protein 34.9g; Carbohydrate 8.1g, of which sugars 3.4g; Fat 24g, of which saturates 9.8g; Cholesterol 114mg; Calcium 70mg; Fibre 1.5g; Sodium 87mg.

LONE STAR STEAK WITH POTATO DINNER

THIS TRADITIONAL AMERICAN MEAL IS USUALLY SERVED WITH CORN ON THE COB, BUT A CRISP, GREEN SALAD WOULD MAKE A LIGHTER ALTERNATIVE ACCOMPANIMENT.

SERVES FOUR

INGREDIENTS
- 45ml/3 tbsp olive oil
- 5 large garlic cloves, crushed
- 5ml/1 tsp coarse black pepper
- 2.5ml/½ tsp ground allspice
- 5ml/1 tsp ground cumin
- 2.5ml/½ tsp chilli powder
- 10ml/2 tsp dried oregano
- 15ml/1 tbsp cider vinegar
- 4 boneless sirloin steaks, about 2cm/¾ in thick
- salt

To serve
- tomato salsa
- freshly cooked corn on the cob (optional)

For the potatoes
- 50ml/2fl oz/¼ cup vegetable oil
- 1 onion, chopped
- 5ml/1 tsp salt
- 900g/2lb potatoes, boiled and diced
- 30–75ml/2–5 tbsp chopped canned or bottled green chillies, according to taste

1 Heat the olive oil in a heavy frying pan. When hot, add the garlic and cook, stirring frequently, for about 3 minutes, until tender and just brown. Do not let the garlic burn, as it will become bitter.

2 Transfer the garlic and oil to a shallow dish large enough to hold the steaks in a single layer.

3 Add the pepper, allspice, cumin, chilli powder, oregano and vinegar to the garlic and stir to blend thoroughly. If necessary, add just enough water to obtain a fairly thick paste.

4 Add the steaks to the dish and turn to coat evenly on both sides with the spice mixture. Cover and leave to marinate for 2 hours or place in the refrigerator overnight. Bring the steaks to room temperature 30 minutes before cooking.

5 To make the potatoes, heat the oil in a large non-stick frying pan. Add the onion and salt. Cook over a medium heat for 5 minutes, until softened. Add the potatoes and chillies. Cook, stirring occasionally, for 15–20 minutes.

6 Season the steaks on both sides with salt to taste. Heat a ridged griddle pan. When hot, add the steaks and cook, turning once, until done to your taste. Allow about 1–2 minutes on each side for rare, 2–3 minutes for medium-rare, and 3–4 minutes for well done.

7 If necessary, briefly reheat the potatoes. Serve immediately, with the tomato salsa and corn, if using.

VARIATION
The steaks can also be cooked on a barbecue. Prepare the fire, and when the coals are glowing red and covered with grey ash, spread them in a single layer. Cook the steaks in the centre of an oiled grill rack set about 13cm/5in above the coals for 1 minute per side to sear them. Move them away from the centre and cook for 10–12 minutes, or longer for medium-rare, turning once.

Per portion: Energy 560Kcal/2346kJ; Protein 45.4g; Carbohydrate 39.2g, of which sugars 5g; Fat 25.6g, of which saturates 5.9g; Cholesterol 89mg; Calcium 32mg; Fibre 2.8g; Sodium 640mg.

TURKEY PATTIES

MINCED TURKEY MAKES DELICIOUSLY LIGHT PATTIES, WHICH ARE IDEAL FOR SUMMER MEALS. SERVE IN SPLIT AND TOASTED BUNS OR PIECES OF CRUSTY BREAD, WITH CHUTNEY, SALAD AND CHUNKY FRIES.

SERVES SIX

INGREDIENTS

675g/1½lb minced (ground) turkey
1 small red onion, finely chopped
grated rind and juice of 1 lime
small handful of fresh thyme leaves
15–30ml/1–2 tbsp olive oil
salt and ground black pepper

VARIATIONS

• You could try chopped fresh oregano, parsley or basil in place of the thyme, and lemon rind instead of lime.
• Substitute minced (ground) chicken, lamb or beef for the turkey.

1 Mix together the turkey, onion, lime rind and juice, thyme and seasoning. Cover and chill for up to 4 hours to allow the flavours to infuse, then divide the mixture into six equal portions and shape into round patties.

2 Preheat a griddle pan. Brush the patties with oil, then place them on the pan and cook for 10–12 minutes. Turn the patties over, brush with more oil and cook for 10–12 minutes on the second side, or until cooked through.

Per portion: Energy 141Kcal/596kJ; Protein 24.8g; Carbohydrate 0.8g, of which sugars 0.6g; Fat 4.4g, of which saturates 1.1g; Cholesterol 69mg; Calcium 15mg; Fibre 0.2g; Sodium 62mg.

TURKEY BREASTS <u>WITH</u> TOMATO-CORN SALSA

ALTHOUGH AN ECONOMICAL AND USEFUL MEAT, TURKEY CAN BE DISAPPOINTINGLY BLAND, SO MARINATING IT BEFORE COOKING AND SERVING WITH A SPICY SALSA IS THE IDEAL APPROACH.

SERVES FOUR

INGREDIENTS
  4 skinless boneless turkey breast
    halves, about 175g/6oz each
  30ml/2 tbsp fresh lemon juice
  30ml/2 tbsp olive oil
  2.5ml/½ tsp ground cumin
  2.5ml/½ tsp dried oregano
  5ml/1 tsp coarse black pepper
  salt
For the salsa
  1 fresh hot green chilli
  450g/1lb tomatoes, seeded
    and chopped
  250g/9oz/1½ cups corn kernels,
    freshly cooked or thawed frozen
  3 spring onions (scallions), chopped
  15ml/1 tbsp chopped fresh parsley
  30ml/2 tbsp chopped fresh
    coriander (cilantro)
  30ml/2 tbsp fresh lemon juice
  45ml/3 tbsp olive oil
  5ml/1 tsp salt

1 With a meat mallet, pound the turkey breasts between two sheets of greaseproof (waxed) paper until thin.

2 In a shallow dish, combine the lemon juice, oil, cumin, oregano and pepper. Add the turkey and turn to coat. Cover and marinate for at least 2 hours, or overnight in the refrigerator.

COOK'S TIP
Use the flat side of a meat mallet to pound the turkey. If you don't have a meat mallet, use the side of a wooden rolling pin.

3 For the salsa, roast the chilli over a gas flame, holding it with tongs, until charred on all sides. Alternatively, char the skin under the hot grill (broiler). Leave to cool for 5 minutes. Wearing rubber gloves, carefully rub off the charred skin. For a less hot flavour, discard the seeds. Chop the chilli finely and place in a bowl.

4 Add the remaining salsa ingredients and toss well to blend. Set aside.

5 Remove the turkey from the marinade. Season lightly on both sides with salt to taste.

6 Heat a ridged griddle pan. When hot, add the turkey breasts and cook for about 3 minutes, until browned on the undersides. Turn and cook the meat on the other side for a further 3–4 minutes, until it is cooked through. Serve the turkey immediately, accompanied by tomato-corn salsa.

VARIATION
Use the cooked turkey, thinly sliced and combined with the salsa, as a filling for warmed flour tortillas.

Per portion: Energy 407Kcal/1711kJ; Protein 45.7g; Carbohydrate 20.6g, of which sugars 9.9g; Fat 16.4g, of which saturates 2.7g; Cholesterol 100mg; Calcium 36mg; Fibre 2.5g; Sodium 761mg.

Stews, Curries Casseroles & Stove-top dishes

It is amazing how many main meals can be cooked entirely on top of the stove, from Classic Fish and Chips to steamed Sea Bass with Orange and Chilli Salsa. Slow food is enjoying a renaissance as more and more people take time to make — and enjoy — delectable stews, curries and casseroles. It's almost mystical, the way disparate ingredients are transformed by slow cooking into a dish in which all the different flavours blend to create a harmonious whole.

ITALIAN FISH STEW

THIS ROBUST FISH AND TOMATO STEW COMES FROM ITALY WHERE IT IS KNOWN AS BRODETTO.

3 To prepare the squid, twist the head and tentacles away from the body. Cut the head from the tentacles. Discard the body contents and peel away the mottled skin. Wash the tentacles and bodies and dry on kitchen paper.

4 Scrub the mussels, discarding any that are damaged or open ones that do not close when sharply tapped.

5 Plunge the tomatoes into boiling water for 30 seconds, then refresh in cold water. Peel off the skins and chop the flesh coarsely.

6 Heat the oil in a large sauté pan. Add the sliced onion and the garlic, and cook gently for 3 minutes. Add the squid and the uncooked white fish, which you reserved earlier, and cook quickly on all sides. Remove the fish from the pan using a slotted spoon.

7 Add 475ml/16fl oz/2 cups strained reserved fish stock, the saffron and tomatoes to the pan. Pour in the wine. Bring to the boil, then reduce the heat and simmer for about 5 minutes. Add the mussels, cover, and cook for 3–4 minutes, until the mussels have opened. Discard any mussels that remain closed.

8 Season the sauce with salt and pepper and put all the fish in the pan. Cook gently for 5 minutes. Sprinkle with the parsley and serve with the croûtons.

SERVES FOUR TO FIVE

INGREDIENTS
    900g/2lb mixture of fish fillets or
    steaks, such as monkfish, cod,
    haddock or hake
    900g/2lb mixture of conger eel,
    red or grey mullet, snapper or
    small white fish, prepared
    according to type
    1 onion, halved
    1 celery stick, coarsely chopped
    225g/8oz squid
    225g/8oz fresh mussels
    675g/1½lb ripe tomatoes
    60ml/4 tbsp olive oil
    1 large onion, thinly sliced
    3 garlic cloves, crushed
    5ml/1 tsp saffron threads
    150ml/¼ pint/⅔ cup dry white wine
    90ml/6 tbsp chopped fresh parsley
    salt and ground black pepper
    croûtons, to serve

1 Remove any skin and bones from the fish fillets or steaks, cut the fish into large pieces and reserve. Place the bones in a pan with all the remaining fish.

2 Add the halved onion and the celery and just cover with water. Bring almost to the boil, then reduce the heat and simmer gently for about 30 minutes. Lift out the fish and remove the flesh from the bones. Strain the stock.

Per portion: Energy 624Kcal/2624kJ; Protein 98.6g; Carbohydrate 12.6g, of which sugars 9.7g; Fat 17.5g, of which saturates 2.9g; Cholesterol 322mg; Calcium 163mg; Fibre 2.8g; Sodium 448mg.

CURRIED PRAWNS IN COCONUT MILK

A WONDERFULLY QUICK AND EASY DISH, THIS FEATURES PRAWNS IN A SPICY YELLOW CURRY GRAVY.

SERVES FOUR TO SIX

INGREDIENTS
600ml/1 pint/2½ cups coconut milk
30ml/2 tbsp yellow curry paste (see
   Cook's Tip)
15ml/1 tbsp Thai fish sauce
2.5ml/½ tsp salt
5ml/1 tsp sugar
450g/1lb raw king prawns (jumbo
   shrimp) peeled, thawed if frozen
225g/8oz cherry tomatoes
yellow and orange (bell) peppers,
   seeded and cut into thin strips,
   chives and juice of ½ lime,
   to garnish

VARIATION
Use cooked prawns (shrimp) for an even
quicker version. Add after the tomatoes
and heat through for 1–2 minutes.

1 Put half the coconut milk in a wok or
pan and bring to the boil. Add the
yellow curry paste, stir until it disperses,
then lower the heat and simmer for
about 10 minutes.

2 Add the Thai fish sauce, salt, sugar
and remaining coconut milk to the
sauce. Simmer for 5 minutes more.

3 Add the prawns and cherry tomatoes.
Simmer very gently for about 5 minutes,
until the prawns are pink and tender.

4 Spoon into a serving dish, sprinkle
with lime juice and garnish with strips
of yellow peppers and chives.

COOK'S TIP
To make yellow curry paste, put into a
food processor or blender 6–8 fresh
yellow chillies, the chopped base of
1 lemon grass stalk, 4 chopped shallots,
4 chopped garlic cloves, 15ml/1 tbsp
chopped peeled fresh root ginger, 5ml/
1 tsp coriander seeds, 5ml/1 tsp mustard
powder, 5ml/1 tsp salt, 2.5ml/½ tsp
ground cinnamon, 15ml/1 tbsp light
brown sugar and 30ml/2 tbsp sunflower
oil. Process to a paste, scrape into a jar,
cover and keep in the refrigerator.

Per portion: Energy 160Kcal/679kJ; Protein 21.5g; Carbohydrate 15.8g, of which sugars 15.5g; Fat 1.7g, of which saturates 0.6g; Cholesterol 219mg; Calcium 144mg; Fibre 2g; Sodium 584mg.

CHINESE-STYLE STEAMED FISH

THIS IS A CLASSIC CHINESE WAY OF COOKING WHOLE FISH, WITH GARLIC, SPRING ONIONS, GINGER AND BLACK BEANS. SERVE WITH BOILED RICE AND SOME STIR-FRIED CHINESE GREENS.

SERVES FOUR TO SIX

INGREDIENTS

2 sea bass, or trout, each weighing about 675–800g/1½–1¾lb
25ml/1½ tbsp salted black beans
2.5ml/½ tsp sugar
30ml/2 tbsp finely shredded fresh root ginger
4 garlic cloves, thinly sliced
30ml/2 tbsp Chinese rice wine or dry sherry
30ml/2 tbsp light soy sauce
4–6 spring onions (scallions), finely shredded or sliced diagonally
45ml/3 tbsp groundnut (peanut) oil
10ml/2 tsp sesame oil

1 Wash the fish inside and out under cold running water, then pat them dry on kitchen paper. Using a sharp knife, slash three or four deep cross shapes on each side of each fish.

2 Mash half the black beans with the sugar in a small bowl and then stir in the remaining whole beans.

3 Place a little ginger and garlic inside the cavity of each fish and then lay them on a plate or dish that will fit inside a large steamer. Rub the bean mixture into the fish, especially into the slashes, then sprinkle the remaining ginger and garlic over the top. Cover and chill for 30 minutes.

4 Place the steamer over a pan of boiling water. Sprinkle the rice wine or sherry and half the soy sauce over the fish and steam them for 15–20 minutes, or until just cooked.

5 Sprinkle with the remaining soy sauce and sprinkle the spring onions over the fish.

6 In a small pan, heat the groundnut oil until smoking, then trickle it over the spring onions. Sprinkle with the sesame oil and serve immediately.

Per portion: Energy 415Kcal/1741kJ; Protein 54.7g; Carbohydrate 1.6g, of which sugars 1.5g; Fat 20.3g, of which saturates 4.3g; Cholesterol 224mg; Calcium 90mg; Fibre 0.2g; Sodium 739mg.

SEA BASS WITH ORANGE CHILLI SALSA

THE CHILLI CITRUS SALSA HAS A FRESHNESS WHICH PROVIDES THE PERFECT CONTRAST TO THE WONDERFUL FLAVOUR OF FRESH SEA BASS.

SERVES FOUR

INGREDIENTS
   4 sea bass fillets
   salt and ground black pepper
   fresh coriander (cilantro), to garnish
For the salsa
   2 fresh green chillies
   2 oranges or pink grapefruit
   1 small onion

1 Make the salsa. Roast the chillies in a dry griddle pan until the skins are blistered, being careful not to let the flesh burn. Put them in a strong plastic bag and tie the top to keep the steam in. Set aside for 20 minutes.

COOK'S TIP
If the fish has not been scaled, do this by running the back of a small filleting knife against the grain of the scales. They should come away cleanly. Rinse and pat dry with kitchen paper.

2 Slice the top and bottom off each orange or grapefruit and cut off all the peel and pith. Cut between the membranes and put each segment in a bowl.

3 Remove the chillies from the bag and peel off the skins. Cut off the stalks, then slit the chillies and scrape out the seeds. Chop the flesh finely. Cut the onion in half and slice it thinly. Add the onion and chillies to the orange pieces and mix lightly. Season and chill.

4 Season the sea bass fillets. Line a steamer with greaseproof (waxed) paper, allowing extra to hang over the sides to help lift out the fish after cooking. Place the empty steamer over a pan of water and bring to the boil.

5 Place the fish in a single layer in the steamer. Cover with a lid and steam for about 8 minutes, or until just cooked. Garnish with fresh coriander and serve with the salsa and a vegetable side dish of your choice.

Per portion: Energy 181Kcal/763kJ; Protein 30.2g; Carbohydrate 6.6g, of which sugars 6.3g; Fat 3.9g, of which saturates 0.6g; Cholesterol 120mg; Calcium 232mg; Fibre 1.3g; Sodium 108mg.

CLASSIC FISH AND CHIPS

*NOTHING BEATS A PIECE OF COD COOKED TO A CRISP WITH FRESHLY MADE CHIPS ON THE SIDE.
THE BATTER SHOULD BE LIGHT AND CRISP, BUT NOT TOO GREASY AND THE FISH SHOULD MELT
IN THE MOUTH. SERVE WITH LEMON WEDGES OR LIME WEDGES IF YOU REALLY WANT TO SHOW OFF.
THE SECRET OF COOKING FISH AND CHIPS SUCCESSFULLY IS TO MAKE SURE THE OIL IS FRESH AND
CLEAN. HEAT THE OIL TO THE CORRECT TEMPERATURE BEFORE COOKING THE CHIPS AND AGAIN
BEFORE YOU ADD THE FISH. SERVE THE DISH IMMEDIATELY, WHILE STILL CRISP AND PIPING HOT.*

SERVES FOUR

INGREDIENTS
  450g/1lb potatoes
  groundnut (peanut) oil for deep-frying
  4 x 175g/6oz cod fillets, skinned
For the batter
  75g/3oz/⅔ cup plain (all-
    purpose) flour
  1 egg yolk
  10ml/2 tsp oil
  175ml/6fl oz/¾ cup water
  salt

1 Cut the potatoes into 5mm/¼in thick
slices. Cut each slice again to make
5mm/¼in chips (French fries).

2 Heat the oil in a deep-fryer to 180°C/
350°F. Add the chips to the fryer and
cook for 3 minutes, then remove from
the pan and shake off all fat and set
to one side.

3 To make the batter, sift the flour
into a bowl and add the remaining
ingredients with a pinch of salt. Beat
well until smooth. Set aside until
ready to use.

4 Cook the chips again in the fat for a
further 5 minutes or so, until they are
really nice and crisp. Drain on kitchen
paper and season with salt. Keep hot in
a low oven while you cook the pieces
of fish.

VARIATION
Although cod is the traditional choice for
fish and chips, you can also use
haddock. Rock salmon, sometimes sold
as huss or dogfish, also has a good
flavour. It has a central length of
cartilage which cannot be removed
before cooking – otherwise the pieces of
fish will fall apart – but can be easily
prised out once the fish is served.

5 Dip the fish into the batter, making
sure they are evenly coated, and shake
off any excess.

6 Carefully lower the fish into the fat
and cook for 5 minutes. Drain on
kitchen paper. Serve with lemon wedges
and the chips.

COOK'S TIPS
• Use fresh rather than frozen fish
for the very best texture and flavour.
If you have to use frozen fish, thaw it
thoroughly and make sure it is dry
before coating with batter.
• Ideally, you should use fresh oil for
deep-frying each time, but it can usually
be safely re-used once more. Do not use
the same oil repeatedly, as it gradually
breaks down and will smoke or even
ignite quite easily. Long storage may
cause it to turn rancid. After the first
use, cool, then strain the oil to remove
any debris. Remember, too, that the oil
will be flavoured, to some extent, by the
food first cooked in it.
• People keeping an eye on their fat
intake may not realize that deep-fried
foods absorb less fat during cooking than
shallow-fried foods. This is because the
initial submersion in the oil, providing
it has been heated to the correct
temperature, quickly seals the outside,
preventing any more fat from being
absorbed by the food.

Per portion: Energy 740Kcal/3093kJ; Protein 32.8g; Carbohydrate 61g, of which sugars 0.8g; Fat 42.2g, of which saturates 4.2g; Cholesterol 0mg; Calcium 134mg; Fibre 3.6g; Sodium 313mg.

GREEN FISH CURRY

ANY FIRM-FLESHED FISH CAN BE USED FOR THIS DELICIOUS CURRY, WHICH GAINS ITS RICH COLOUR FROM A MIXTURE OF FRESH HERBS; TRY EXOTICS, SUCH AS SWORDFISH OR COLEY.

1 First make the curry paste. Combine the garlic, fresh root ginger, green chillies, the lime juice and shrimp paste in a food processor. Add the coriander seeds and five-spice powder, with half the sesame oil. Process to a fine paste, then set aside until required.

2 Heat a wok or large shallow pan and pour in the remaining sesame oil. When it is hot, stir-fry the red onions over a high heat for 2 minutes. Add the fish and stir-fry for 1–2 minutes to seal the fillets on all sides.

3 Lift out the red onions and fish and put them on a plate. Add the curry paste to the wok or pan and cook for 1 minute, stirring. Return the fish and red onions to the wok or pan, pour in the coconut milk and bring to the boil. Lower the heat, add the Thai fish sauce and simmer for 5–7 minutes, until the fish is cooked through.

SERVES FOUR

INGREDIENTS
4 garlic cloves, coarsely chopped
5cm/2in piece fresh root ginger,
 peeled and coarsely chopped
2 fresh green chillies, seeded and
 coarsely chopped
grated rind and juice of 1 lime
5–10ml/1–2 tsp shrimp paste
5ml/1 tsp coriander seeds
5ml/1 tsp five-spice powder
75ml/5 tbsp sesame oil
2 red onions, finely chopped
900g/2lb hoki fillets, skinned
400ml/14fl oz/1²⁄₃ cups coconut milk

45ml/3 tbsp Thai fish sauce
50g/2oz fresh coriander
 (cilantro) leaves
50g/2oz fresh mint leaves
50g/2oz fresh basil leaves
6 spring onions (scallions), chopped
150ml/¼ pint/²⁄₃ cup sunflower oil
sliced fresh green chilli and finely
 chopped fresh coriander (cilantro),
 to garnish
cooked rice and lime wedges,
 to serve

COOK'S TIP
Shrimp paste, also known as blachan or terasi, is available in Asian food stores.

4 Meanwhile, process the herbs, spring onions, lime rind and oil in a food processor to a coarse paste. Stir into the fish curry. Garnish with chilli and coriander and serve with rice and lime wedges.

Per portion: Energy 608Kcal/2527kJ; Protein 41g; Carbohydrate 13.3g, of which sugars 9.5g; Fat 43.8g, of which saturates 5.9g; Cholesterol 0mg; Calcium 168mg; Fibre 1.3g; Sodium 313mg.

LAMB AND NEW POTATO CURRY

THIS DISH MAKES THE MOST OF AN ECONOMICAL CUT OF MEAT BY COOKING IT SLOWLY UNTIL THE MEAT IS FALLING FROM THE BONE. CHILLIES AND COCONUT CREAM GIVE IT LOTS OF FLAVOUR.

SERVES FOUR

INGREDIENTS

25g/1oz/2 tbsp butter
4 garlic cloves, crushed
2 onions, sliced into rings
2.5ml/½ tsp each ground cumin,
  ground coriander, turmeric and
  cayenne pepper
2–3 fresh red chillies, seeded and
  finely chopped
300ml/½ pint/1¼ cups hot
  chicken stock
200ml/7fl oz/scant 1 cup
  coconut cream
4 lamb shanks, trimmed of fat
450g/1lb new potatoes, halved
6 ripe tomatoes, quartered
salt and ground black pepper
fresh coriander (cilantro) leaves,
  to garnish
spicy rice, to serve

2 Stir in the hot stock and coconut cream. Place the lamb shanks in the liquid and cover the casserole with foil. Cook in the oven for 2 hours, turning the shanks twice, first after about an hour or so and again about half an hour later.

3 Par-boil the potatoes for 10 minutes, drain and add to the casserole with the tomatoes, then cook uncovered in the oven for a further 35 minutes. Season to taste, garnish with coriander leaves and serve with the spicy rice.

1 Preheat the oven to 160ºC/325ºF/ Gas 3. Melt the butter in a large flameproof casserole, add the garlic and onions and cook over a low heat for 15 minutes, until golden. Stir in the cumin, ground coriander, turmeric, cayenne and chillies, then cook for a further 2 minutes.

COOK'S TIP
Make this dish a day in advance if possible. Cool and chill overnight, then it will be easy to skim off the excess fat that has risen to the surface and solidified. Reheat the curry thoroughly before you serve it.

Per portion: Energy 364Kcal/1528kJ; Protein 23.5g; Carbohydrate 30.5g, of which sugars 12.1g; Fat 17.4g, of which saturates 8.8g; Cholesterol 89mg; Calcium 58mg; Fibre 3.5g; Sodium 205mg.

LAMB STEW WITH SHALLOTS AND NEW POTATOES

THIS FRESH LEMON-SEASONED STEW IS FINISHED WITH AN ITALIAN MIXTURE OF CHOPPED GARLIC, PARSLEY AND LEMON RIND KNOWN AS GREMOLATA, THE TRADITIONAL TOPPING FOR OSSO BUCCO.

SERVES SIX

INGREDIENTS

1kg/2¼lb boneless shoulder of lamb,
  trimmed of fat and cut into 5cm/
  2in cubes
1 garlic clove, finely chopped
finely grated rind of ½ lemon and
  juice of 1 lemon
90ml/6 tbsp olive oil
45ml/3 tbsp plain (all-purpose) flour
1 large onion, sliced
5 anchovy fillets in olive oil, drained
2.5ml/½ tsp caster (superfine) sugar
300ml/½ pint/1¼ cups white wine
475ml/16fl oz/2 cups lamb stock or
  half stock and half water
1 fresh bay leaf
fresh thyme sprig
fresh parsley sprig
500g/1¼lb small new potatoes
250g/9oz shallots, peeled but
  left whole
45ml/3 tbsp double (heavy)
  cream (optional)
salt and ground black pepper
For the gremolata
1 garlic clove, finely chopped
finely shredded rind of ½ lemon
45ml/3 tbsp chopped fresh flat
  leaf parsley

1 Mix the lamb with the garlic and the rind and juice of ½ lemon. Season with pepper and mix in 15ml/1 tbsp olive oil, then leave to marinate for 12–24 hours.

2 Drain the lamb, reserving the marinade, and pat the lamb dry with kitchen paper. Preheat the oven to 180°C/350°F/Gas 4.

COOK'S TIP

A mezzaluna (double-handled, half-moon shaped, curved chopping blade) makes a very good job of chopping gremolata ingredients. If using a food processor or electric chopper, take care not to overprocess the mixture as it is easy to reduce the ingredients to a paste.

3 Heat 30ml/2 tbsp olive oil in a large, heavy frying pan. Season the flour with salt and pepper and toss the lamb in it to coat, shaking off any excess. Seal the lamb on all sides in the hot oil. Do this in batches, transferring each batch of lamb to an ovenproof pan or flameproof casserole as you brown it. You may need to add an extra 15ml/1 tbsp olive oil to the pan.

4 Reduce the heat, add another 15ml/1 tbsp oil to the pan and cook the onion gently over a very low heat, stirring frequently, for 10 minutes, until softened and golden but not browned. Add the anchovies and caster sugar and cook, mashing the anchovies into the soft onion with a wooden spoon.

5 Add the reserved marinade, increase the heat a little and cook for about 1–2 minutes, then pour in the wine and stock or stock and water and bring to the boil. Simmer gently for about 5 minutes, then pour over the lamb.

6 Tie the bay leaf, thyme and parsley together and add to the lamb. Season with salt and pepper, then cover tightly and cook in the oven for 1 hour. Stir the potatoes into the stew and cook for a further 20 minutes.

7 Meanwhile, to make the gremolata, chop all the ingredients together finely. Place in a dish, cover and set aside.

8 Heat the remaining oil in a frying pan and brown the shallots on all sides, then stir them into the lamb. Cover and cook for a further 30–40 minutes, until the lamb is tender. Transfer the lamb and vegetables to a dish and keep warm. Discard the herbs.

9 Boil the cooking juices to reduce and concentrate them, then add the cream, if using, and simmer for 2–3 minutes. Adjust the seasoning, adding a little lemon juice to taste. Pour this sauce over the lamb, sprinkle the gremolata on top and serve immediately.

Per portion: Energy 553Kcal/2311kJ; Protein 37g; Carbohydrate 26.2g, of which sugars 5.3g; Fat 30.6g, of which saturates 10.4g; Cholesterol 128mg; Calcium 79mg; Fibre 2.7g; Sodium 261mg.

TACOS <u>WITH</u> SHREDDED BEEF

IN MEXICO, TACOS ARE MOST OFTEN MADE WITH SOFT CORN TORTILLAS, WHICH ARE FILLED AND FOLDED IN HALF. IT IS UNUSUAL TO SEE THE CRISP SHELLS OF CORN WHICH ARE SO WIDELY USED IN TEX-MEX COOKING. TACOS ARE ALWAYS EATEN IN THE HAND.

SERVES SIX

INGREDIENTS
    450g/1lb rump (round) steak, diced
    150g/5oz/1 cup masa harina
    2.5ml/½ tsp salt
    120ml/4fl oz/½ cup warm water
    10ml/2 tsp dried oregano
    5ml/1 tsp ground cumin
    30ml/2 tbsp oil
    1 onion, thinly sliced
    2 garlic cloves, crushed
    fresh coriander (cilantro), to garnish
    shredded lettuce, lime wedges and
        tomato salsa, to serve

1 Put the steak in a deep frying pan and pour over water to cover. Bring to the boil, then lower the heat and simmer for 1–1½ hours.

2 Meanwhile, make the tortilla dough. Mix the masa harina and salt in a large mixing bowl. Add the warm water, a little at a time, to make a dough that can be worked into a ball. Knead the dough on a lightly floured surface for 3–4 minutes until smooth, then wrap the dough in clear film (plastic wrap) and leave to rest for 1 hour.

3 Put the meat on a board, let it cool slightly, then shred it, using two forks. Put the meat in a bowl. Divide the tortilla dough into six equal balls.

4 Open a tortilla press and line both sides with plastic (this can be cut from a new plastic sandwich bag). Put each ball on the press and flatten it into a 15–20cm/6–8in round.

5 Heat a griddle or frying pan until hot. Cook each tortilla for 15–20 seconds on each side, and then for a further 15 seconds on the first side. Keep the tortillas warm and soft by folding them inside a slightly damp dishtowel.

6 Add the oregano and cumin to the shredded meat and mix well. Heat the oil in a frying pan and cook the onion and garlic for 3–4 minutes, until softened. Add the meat mixture and toss over the heat until heated through.

7 Place some shredded lettuce on a tortilla, top with shredded beef and salsa, fold in half and serve with lime wedges. Garnish with fresh coriander.

Per portion: Energy 232Kcal/975kJ; Protein 18.6g; Carbohydrate 21.4g, of which sugars 1.8g; Fat 8.6g, of which saturates 2.6g; Cholesterol 46mg; Calcium 44mg; Fibre 1.1g; Sodium 198mg.

CHILLI CON CARNE

ORIGINALLY MADE WITH FINELY CHOPPED BEEF, CHILLIES AND KIDNEY BEANS BY HUNGRY LABOURERS WORKING ON THE TEXAN RAILROAD, THIS FAMOUS STEW HAS BECOME AN INTERNATIONAL FAVOURITE.

SERVES EIGHT

INGREDIENTS

  1.2kg/2½lb lean braising steak
  30ml/2 tbsp sunflower oil
  1 large onion, chopped
  2 garlic cloves, finely chopped
  15ml/1 tbsp plain (all-purpose) flour
  300ml/½ pint/1¼ cups red wine
  300ml/½ pint/1¼ cups beef stock
  30ml/2 tbsp tomato purée (paste)
  fresh coriander (cilantro) leaves
  salt and ground black pepper
For the beans
  30ml/2 tbsp olive oil
  1 onion, chopped
  1 red chilli, seeded and chopped
  2 x 400g/14oz cans red kidney
    beans, drained and rinsed
  400g/14oz can chopped tomatoes
For the topping
  6 tomatoes, peeled and chopped
  1 green chilli, seeded and chopped
  30ml/2 tbsp chopped fresh chives
  30ml/2 tbsp fresh coriander (cilantro)
  150ml/¼ pint/⅔ cup sour cream

2 Use a slotted spoon to remove the onion from the pan, then add the floured beef and cook over a high heat until browned on all sides. Remove from the pan and set aside, then flour and brown another batch of meat.

3 When the last batch of meat is browned, return the first batches with the onion to the pan. Stir in the wine, stock and tomato purée. Bring to the boil, reduce the heat and simmer for 45 minutes, or until the beef is tender.

4 Meanwhile, for the beans, heat the olive oil in a frying pan and cook the onion and chilli until softened. Add the kidney beans and tomatoes and simmer gently for 20–25 minutes, or until thickened and reduced.

5 Mix the tomatoes, chilli, chives and coriander for the topping. Ladle the meat mixture on to warmed plates. Add a layer of bean mixture and tomato topping. Finish with sour cream and garnish with coriander leaves.

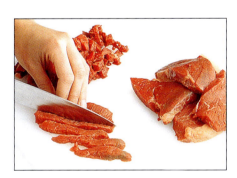

1 Cut the meat into thick strips and then cut it crossways into small cubes. Heat the oil in a large, flameproof casserole. Add the chopped onion and garlic, and cook until softened but not coloured. Meanwhile, season the flour and place it on a plate, then toss a batch of meat in it.

VARIATION
This stew is equally good served with tortillas instead of rice. Wrap the tortillas in foil and warm through in the oven.

Per portion: Energy 470Kcal/1969kJ; Protein 42g; Carbohydrate 28.4g, of which sugars 11.2g; Fat 18.9g, of which saturates 6.9g; Cholesterol 106mg; Calcium 124mg; Fibre 8.2g; Sodium 517mg.

RED CHICKEN CURRY WITH BAMBOO SHOOTS

BAMBOO SHOOTS HAVE A LOVELY CRUNCHY TEXTURE. IT IS QUITE ACCEPTABLE TO USE CANNED ONES, AS FRESH BAMBOO IS NOT READILY AVAILABLE IN THE WEST. BUY CANNED WHOLE BAMBOO SHOOTS, WHICH ARE CRISPER AND OF BETTER QUALITY THAN SLICED SHOOTS. RINSE BEFORE USING.

SERVES FOUR TO SIX

INGREDIENTS
   1 litre/1¾ pints/4 cups coconut milk
   450g/1lb skinless, chicken
      breast fillets, cut into bitesize
      pieces
   30ml/2 tbsp Thai fish sauce
   15ml/1 tbsp sugar
   225g/8oz drained canned bamboo
      shoots, rinsed and sliced
   5 kaffir lime leaves, torn
   salt and ground black pepper
   chopped fresh red chillies and
      kaffir lime leaves, to garnish
For the red curry paste
   5ml/1 tsp coriander seeds
   2.5ml/½ tsp cumin seeds
   12–15 fresh red chillies, seeded
      and coarsely chopped
   4 shallots, thinly sliced
   2 garlic cloves, chopped
   15ml/1 tbsp chopped galangal
   2 lemon grass stalks, chopped
   3 kaffir lime leaves, chopped
   4 fresh coriander (cilantro) roots
   10 black peppercorns
   good pinch of ground cinnamon
   5ml/1 tsp ground turmeric
   2.5ml/½ tsp shrimp paste
   5ml/1 tsp salt
   30ml/2 tbsp vegetable oil

1 Make the curry paste. Dry-fry the coriander and cumin seeds for 1–2 minutes, then put in a mortar or food processor with the remaining ingredients, except the oil, and pound or process to a paste.

2 Add the oil, a little at a time, mixing or processing well after each addition. Transfer to a jar and keep in the refrigerator until ready to use.

3 Pour half of the coconut milk into a large, heavy pan. Bring the milk to the boil, stirring constantly until it has separated.

4 Stir in 30ml/2 tbsp of the red curry paste and cook the mixture for 2–3 minutes, stirring constantly. The remaining red curry paste can be kept in the refrigerator for up to 3 months.

5 Add the chicken pieces, Thai fish sauce and sugar to the pan. Stir well, then cook for 5–6 minutes, until the chicken changes colour and is cooked through, stirring constantly to prevent the mixture from sticking to the base of the pan.

6 Pour the remaining coconut milk into the pan, then add the sliced bamboo shoots and torn kaffir lime leaves. Bring the curry back to the boil over a medium heat, stirring constantly to prevent the mixture from sticking, then taste and season with salt and pepper if necessary.

7 To serve, spoon the curry into a warmed serving dish and garnish with chopped chillies and kaffir lime leaves. Boiled Thai jasmine rice would be a good accompaniment.

VARIATION
Instead of, or as well as, bamboo shoots, use straw mushrooms. These are available in cans from Asian stores and supermarkets. Drain well and then stir into the curry at the end of the recipe.

COOK'S TIP
It is essential to use chicken breast portions, rather than any other cut, for this curry, as it is cooked very quickly. Look for diced chicken or strips of chicken (which are often labelled "stir-fry chicken") in the supermarket.

Per portion: Energy 261Kcal/1105kJ; Protein 29.6g; Carbohydrate 19.6g, of which sugars 18.3g; Fat 7.8g, of which saturates 1.5g; Cholesterol 79mg; Calcium 95mg; Fibre 1.1g; Sodium 837mg.

ROASTED
& BAKED

Roasting and baking are two of the easiest ways of cooking a

well-balanced meal — and one of the most delicious. The

important thing to remember is that quality really does tell, so

it is worth buying the best organic meat, game, poultry and fish

you can afford. For a dinner with family and friends that is

sure to impress, choose Moussaka or Roasted Vegetables with

Salsa Verde. Smoked Haddock and New Potato Pie is another

excellent choice, and is versatile too, because you can substitute

the fish for salmon, cod or whatever is in season.

ROASTED VEGETABLES <u>WITH</u> SALSA VERDE

THERE ARE ENDLESS VARIATIONS OF THE ITALIAN SALSA VERDE, WHICH MEANS "GREEN SAUCE". USUALLY A BLEND OF FRESH CHOPPED HERBS, GARLIC, OLIVE OIL, ANCHOVIES AND CAPERS, THIS IS A SIMPLIFIED VERSION. HERE, IT IS SERVED WITH VEGETABLES AND A RICE DISH FROM CYPRUS.

SERVES FOUR

INGREDIENTS

   3 courgettes (zucchini),
     sliced lengthways
   1 large fennel bulb, cut
     into wedges
   450g/1lb butternut squash, cut into
     2cm/¾in chunks
   12 shallots
   2 red (bell) peppers, seeded
     and cut lengthways into
     thick slices
   4 plum tomatoes, halved and seeded
   45ml/3 tbsp olive oil
   2 garlic cloves, crushed
   5ml/1 tsp balsamic vinegar
   salt and ground black pepper
For the salsa verde
   45ml/3 tbsp chopped fresh mint
   90ml/6 tbsp chopped fresh flat
     leaf parsley
   15ml/1 tbsp Dijon mustard
   juice of ½ lemon
   30ml/2 tbsp olive oil
For the rice
   15ml/1 tbsp vegetable or olive oil
   75g/3oz/¾ cup vermicelli, broken
     into short lengths
   225g/8oz/generous 1 cup long
     grain rice
   900ml/1½ pints/3¾ cups
     vegetable stock

1 To make the salsa verde, place all the ingredients, with the exception of the olive oil, in a food processor or blender. Blend to a coarse paste, then add the oil, a little at a time, until the mixture forms a smooth purée.

2 Transfer the salsa to a bowl, season to taste with salt and pepper, cover and set aside.

3 Preheat the oven to 220°C/425°F/ Gas 7. To roast the vegetables, toss the courgettes, fennel, squash, shallots, peppers and tomatoes in the olive oil, garlic and balsamic vinegar. Set aside for 10 minutes to allow all the flavours to combine.

4 Place all the vegetables – apart from the squash and tomatoes – on a large baking sheet, brush with half the oil and vinegar mixture and season.

5 Roast the vegetables for 25 minutes, then remove the baking sheet from the oven. Using a fork, turn all the vegetables over and brush with the rest of the oil and vinegar mixture. Add the butternut squash and plum tomatoes, return to the oven and cook for a further 20–25 minutes, until all the vegetables are tender and lightly charred around the edges.

VARIATIONS
• Substitute 45ml/3 tbsp watercress for half the parsley in the salsa.
• Use sherry vinegar instead of balsamic vinegar to flavour the vegetables.
• If you like, add a medium aubergine (eggplant), cut into chunks, to the mixture of roasted vegetables.

6 Meanwhile, prepare the rice. Heat the oil in a heavy pan. Add the vermicelli and cook for about 3 minutes, or until golden and crisp. Season to taste.

7 Rinse the rice under cold running water, then drain well and add it to the vermicelli. Cook for 1 minute, stirring to coat it in the oil.

8 Add the vegetable stock, then cover the pan and allow to cook for about 12 minutes, until all the liquid is absorbed. Stir the rice, then cover and leave to stand for 10 minutes. Serve the warm rice with the roasted vegetables and salsa verde.

COOK'S TIP
The salsa verde will keep for up to 1 week if stored in an airtight container in the refrigerator.

Per portion: Energy 519Kcal/2160kJ; Protein 12.1g; Carbohydrate 75.3g, of which sugars 14.7g; Fat 18.7g, of which saturates 2.8g; Cholesterol 0mg; Calcium 151mg; Fibre 6.9g; Sodium 27mg.

MOUSSAKA

This is a traditional eastern Mediterranean dish, popular in both Greece and Turkey. Layers of minced lamb, aubergines, tomatoes and onions are topped with a creamy yogurt and cheese sauce in this delicious, authentic recipe.

SERVES FOUR

INGREDIENTS
    450g/1lb aubergines (eggplants)
    150ml/¼ pint/⅔ cup olive oil
    1 large onion, chopped
    2–3 garlic cloves, finely chopped
    675g/1½lb lean minced (ground) lamb
    15ml/1 tbsp plain (all-purpose) flour
    400g/14oz can chopped tomatoes
    30ml/2 tbsp chopped fresh herbs
    450g/1lb fresh tomatoes, sliced
    salt and ground black pepper
For the topping
    300ml/½ pint/1¼ cups yogurt
    2 eggs
    25g/1oz feta cheese, crumbled
    25g/1oz/⅓ cup freshly grated
      Parmesan cheese

1 Cut the aubergines into thin slices and layer them in a colander, sprinkling each layer with salt.

2 Cover the aubergines with a plate and a weight, then leave for about 30 minutes. Pat dry with kitchen paper.

3 Heat 45ml/3 tbsp of the oil in a large, heavy pan. Cook the onion and garlic until softened, but not coloured. Add the lamb and cook over a high heat, stirring frequently, until browned.

4 Stir in the flour until mixed, then stir in the canned tomatoes, herbs and seasoning. Bring to the boil, reduce the heat and simmer gently for 20 minutes.

5 Meanwhile, heat a little of the remaining oil in a large frying pan. Add as many aubergine slices as can be laid in the pan in a single layer, then cook until golden on both sides. Set the cooked aubergines aside. Heat more oil and continue cooking the aubergines, in batches, adding oil as necessary.

COOK'S TIP
Salting and drying the aubergines before cooking reduces the amount of fat that they absorb and helps them to brown more quickly.

6 Preheat the oven to 180°C/350°F/ Gas 4. Arrange half the aubergine slices in a large, shallow ovenproof dish, then add a layer of half the fresh tomatoes.

7 Top the slices with about half of the meat and tomato sauce mixture, then add a layer of the remaining aubergine slices, followed by the remaining tomato slices. Spread the remaining meat mixture over the aubergines and tomatoes.

8 Beat together the yogurt and eggs, then mix in the feta and Parmesan cheeses. Pour the mixture over the meat and spread it evenly.

9 Transfer the moussaka to the oven and bake for 35–40 minutes, or until golden and bubbling.

VARIATION
Use large courgettes (zucchini) instead of aubergines (eggplants), if you like. Cut them diagonally into fairly thick slices.

Per portion: Energy 753Kcal/3132kJ; Protein 46.2g; Carbohydrate 19.4g, of which sugars 17.6g; Fat 55.3g, of which saturates 17.6g; Cholesterol 237mg; Calcium 329mg; Fibre 4.9g; Sodium 425mg.

ROASTED COD WITH FRESH TOMATO SAUCE

REALLY FRESH COD HAS A SWEET, DELICATE FLAVOUR AND A PURE WHITE FLAKY FLESH. SERVED WITH AN AROMATIC TOMATO SAUCE, IT MAKES A DELICIOUS MEAL.

SERVES FOUR

INGREDIENTS
   350g/12oz ripe plum tomatoes
   75ml/5 tbsp olive oil
   2.5ml/½ tsp sugar
   2 strips of pared orange rind
   1 fresh thyme sprig
   6 fresh basil leaves
   900g/2lb fresh cod fillet, skin on
   salt and ground black pepper
   steamed green beans, to serve

COOK'S TIP
Cod is becoming increasingly rare and expensive. You can substitute any firm white fish fillets in this dish. Try haddock, pollock, or that excellent and underrated fish, coley. When raw, coley flesh looks grey, but it turns white on cooking.

1 Preheat the oven to 230°C/450°F/ Gas 8. Coarsely chop the tomatoes.

2 Heat 15ml/1 tbsp of the olive oil in a heavy pan, add the tomatoes, sugar, orange rind, thyme and basil, and simmer for about 5 minutes, until the tomatoes are soft.

3 Press the tomato mixture through a fine sieve, discarding the solids that remain in the sieve. Pour into a small pan and heat gently.

4 Scale the cod fillet and cut on the diagonal into four pieces. Season well.

5 Heat the remaining oil in a heavy frying pan and cook the cod, skin side down, until the skin is crisp. Place the fish on a greased baking sheet, skin side up, and roast in the oven for 8–10 minutes, until the fish is cooked through. Serve the fish on the steamed green beans with the tomato sauce.

Per portion: Energy 319Kcal/1330kJ; Protein 41.8g; Carbohydrate 2.7g, of which sugars 2.7g; Fat 15.6g, of which saturates 2.3g; Cholesterol 104mg; Calcium 27mg; Fibre 0.9g; Sodium 143mg.

BACON-WRAPPED TROUT <u>WITH</u> STUFFING

THIS STUFFING IS BASED ON A SCOTTISH SPECIALITY, A MIXTURE OF OATMEAL AND ONION CALLED SKIRLIE. IF TROUT IS NOT READILY AVAILABLE, HERRING CAN BE COOKED IN THE SAME WAY.

SERVES FOUR

INGREDIENTS

    10 dry-cured streaky (fatty) bacon
        rashers (strips)
    40g/1½oz/3 tbsp butter
    1 onion, finely chopped
    115g/4oz/1 cup oatmeal
    30ml/2 tbsp chopped fresh
        parsley
    30ml/2 tbsp chopped fresh
        chives
    4 trout, about 350g/12oz each,
        gutted and boned
    juice of ½ lemon
    salt and ground black pepper
    watercress, cherry tomatoes and
        lemon wedges, to serve
For the herb mayonnaise
    6 watercress sprigs
    15ml/1 tbsp chopped fresh
        chives
    30ml/2 tbsp coarsely
        chopped parsley
    90ml/6 tbsp lemon mayonnaise
    30ml/2 tbsp crème fraîche
    2.5–5ml/½–1 tsp tarragon mustard

1 Preheat oven to 190°C/375°F/Gas 5. Chop two of the bacon rashers. Melt 25g/1oz/2 tbsp of the butter in a large frying pan and cook the bacon briefly. Add the finely chopped onion and cook gently, stirring occasionally, for 5–8 minutes, until softened.

2 Add the oatmeal and cook until the oatmeal darkens and absorbs the fat, but do not allow it to overbrown. Stir in the parsley, chives and seasoning. Cool.

3 Wash and dry the trout, then stuff with the oatmeal mixture. Wrap each fish in two bacon rashers and place in an ovenproof dish. Dot with the remaining butter and sprinkle with the lemon juice. Bake for 20–25 minutes, until the bacon browns and crisps.

4 Meanwhile, make the mayonnaise. Place the watercress, chives and parsley in a sieve and pour boiling water over them. Drain, rinse under cold water, and drain well on kitchen paper.

5 Purée the herbs in a mortar with a pestle. (This is easier than using a food processor for this small quantity.) Stir the puréed herbs into the lemon mayonnaise together with the crème fraîche. Add tarragon mustard to taste and stir to combine.

6 When cooked, transfer the trout to warmed serving plates and serve immediately with watercress, tomatoes and lemon wedges, accompanied by the herb mayonnaise.

Per portion: Energy 870Kcal/3625kJ; Protein 65.9g; Carbohydrate 24.5g, of which sugars 2.6g; Fat 57.1g, of which saturates 17.8g; Cholesterol 300mg; Calcium 115mg; Fibre 2.5g; Sodium 1245mg.

SMOKED HADDOCK AND NEW POTATO PIE

SMOKED HADDOCK HAS A SALTY FLAVOUR AND CAN BE BOUGHT EITHER DYED OR UNDYED. THE DYED FISH HAS A STRONG YELLOW COLOUR, WHILE THE OTHER IS ALMOST CREAMY IN COLOUR.

SERVES FOUR

INGREDIENTS

450g/1lb smoked haddock fillet
475ml/16fl oz/2 cups semi-skimmed
  (low-fat) milk
2 bay leaves
1 onion, quartered
4 cloves
450g/1lb new potatoes
butter, for greasing
30ml/2 tbsp cornflour (cornstarch)
60ml/4 tbsp double (heavy) cream
30ml/2 tbsp chopped fresh chervil
salt and ground black pepper
mixed vegetables, to serve

VARIATIONS

Instead of using all smoked haddock for this pie, use half smoked and half fresh. Cook the two types together, as described in Step 1. A handful of peeled prawns (shrimp) is a good addition to this pie if you want to make it even more filling.

COOK'S TIP

The fish gives out liquid as it cooks, so it is best to start with a slightly thicker sauce than you might think is necessary.

1 Preheat the oven to 200°C/400°F/ Gas 6. Place the haddock in a deep-sided frying pan. Pour the milk over and add the bay leaves.

2 Stud the onion with the cloves and place it in the pan with the fish and milk. Cover the top and simmer for about 10 minutes or until the fish starts to flake.

3 Remove the fish with a slotted spoon and set aside to cool. Strain the liquid from the pan into a separate pan and set aside.

4 To prepare the potatoes, cut them into thin slices, leaving the skins on.

5 Blanch the potatoes in a large pan of lightly salted, boiling water for about 5 minutes. Drain.

6 Grease the base and sides of a 1.2 litre/2 pint/5 cup ovenproof dish. Then using a knife and fork, carefully flake the fish.

7 Reheat the milk in the pan. Mix the cornflour with a little water to form a paste and stir in the cream and the chervil. Add to the milk in the pan and cook until thickened.

8 Arrange one-third of the potatoes over the base of the dish and season with pepper. Lay half of the fish over. Repeat layering, finishing with a layer of potatoes on top.

9 Pour the sauce over the top, making sure that it sinks down through the mixture. Cover with foil and cook for 30 minutes. Remove the foil and cook for a further 10 minutes to brown the surface. Serve immediately with a selection of mixed vegetables.

Per portion: Energy 300Kcal/1266kJ; Protein 23.9g; Carbohydrate 32.4g, of which sugars 1.9g; Fat 9.3g, of which saturates 5.3g; Cholesterol 61mg; Calcium 56mg; Fibre 1.5g; Sodium 881mg.

ROASTED CHICKEN <u>WITH</u> GRAPES <u>AND</u> FRESH ROOT GINGER

THIS DISH, WITH ITS BLEND OF SPICES AND SWEET FRUIT, IS INSPIRED BY MOROCCAN FLAVOURS.
SERVE WITH COUSCOUS, MIXED WITH A HANDFUL OF COOKED CHICKPEAS.

SERVES FOUR

INGREDIENTS

1–1.6kg/2¼–3½lb chicken
115–130g/4–4½oz fresh root
  ginger, grated
6–8 garlic cloves, coarsely chopped
juice of 1 lemon
about 30ml/2 tbsp olive oil
2–3 large pinches of ground cinnamon
500g/1¼lb seeded red and
  green grapes
500g/1¼lb seedless green grapes
5–7 shallots, chopped
about 250ml/8fl oz/1 cup chicken stock
salt and ground black pepper

1 Rub the chicken with half of the ginger, the garlic, half of the lemon juice, the olive oil, cinnamon, salt and lots of pepper. Leave to marinate.

2 Meanwhile, cut the red and green seeded grapes in half, remove the seeds and set aside. Add the whole green seedless grapes to the halved ones.

3 Preheat the oven to 180°C/350°F/ Gas 4. Heat a heavy frying pan or flameproof casserole until hot.

4 Remove the chicken from the marinade, add to the pan and cook until browned on all sides. (There should be enough oil on the chicken to brown it but, if not, add a little extra.)

5 Put some of the shallots into the chicken cavity with the garlic and ginger from the marinade and as many of the red and green grapes that will fit inside. Roast in the oven for 40–60 minutes, or until the chicken is tender.

VARIATIONS
• This dish is good made with duck in place of the chicken. Marinate and roast as above, adding 15–30ml/1–2 tbsp honey to the pan sauce as it cooks.
• Use boneless chicken breast portions, with the skin still attached, instead of a whole chicken. Pan-fry the chicken portions, rather than roasting them.

6 Remove the chicken from the pan and keep warm. Pour off any oil from the pan, reserving any sediment in the base of the pan. Add the remaining shallots to the pan and cook for about 5 minutes until softened.

7 Add half the remaining red and green grapes, the remaining ginger, the stock and any juices from the roast chicken and cook over a medium-high heat until the grapes have cooked down to a thick sauce. Season with salt, ground black pepper and the remaining lemon juice to taste.

8 Serve the chicken on a warmed serving dish, surrounded by the sauce and the reserved grapes.

COOK'S TIP
Seeded Italia or muscat grapes have a delicious, sweet fragrance and are perfect for using in this recipe.

Per portion: Energy 454Kcal/1891kJ; Protein 31.6g; Carbohydrate 19.5g, of which sugars 19.5g; Fat 28.1g, of which saturates 7g; Cholesterol 165mg; Calcium 28mg; Fibre 1g; Sodium 116mg.

SOMERSET CIDER-GLAZED HAM

*WILLIAM THE CONQUEROR INTRODUCED CIDER MAKING TO ENGLAND FROM NORMANDY IN 1066.
THIS WONDERFUL OLD WEST-COUNTRY HAM GLAZED WITH CIDER IS TRADITIONALLY SERVED WITH
CRANBERRY SAUCE AND IS IDEAL FOR CHRISTMAS FEASTING.*

SERVES EIGHT TO TEN

INGREDIENTS
    2kg/4½lb middle gammon
      (cured ham) in a single piece
    1.3 litres/2¼ pints/5⅔ cups medium-
      dry (hard) cider
    1 large or 2 small onions
    about 30 whole cloves
    3 bay leaves
    10 black peppercorns
    45ml/3 tbsp soft light brown sugar
    bunch of flat leaf parsley, to garnish
For the cranberry sauce
    2 clementines
    350g/12oz/3 cups cranberries
    175g/6oz/¾ cup soft light brown sugar
    30ml/2 tbsp port

1 Weigh the ham and calculate the
cooking time at 20 minutes per 450g/
1lb, then place it in a large casserole or
pan. Stud the onion or onions with
5–10 of the cloves and add to the
casserole or pan with the bay leaves
and peppercorns.

2 Add 1.2 litres/2 pints/5 cups of the
cider and enough water just to cover
the ham. Heat until simmering and then
carefully skim off the scum that rises to
the surface using a large spoon or ladle.
Start timing the cooking from the
moment the stock begins to simmer.

VARIATION
Use honey in place of the soft brown
sugar for the glaze and serve the ham
with redcurrant sauce or jelly.

3 Cover with a lid or foil and simmer
gently for the calculated time. Towards
the end of the cooking time, preheat the
oven to 220°C/425°F/Gas 7.

4 Heat the sugar and remaining cider in
a pan; stir until the sugar has dissolved.

5 Simmer for 5 minutes to make a dark,
sticky glaze. Remove the pan from the
heat and leave to cool for 5 minutes.

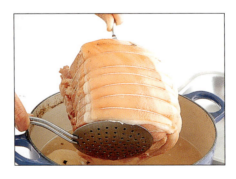

6 Lift the ham out of the casserole or
pan using a slotted spoon and a large
fork. Carefully and evenly, cut the rind
from the ham, then score the fat into a
neat diamond pattern. Place the ham in
a roasting pan or ovenproof dish.

7 Press a clove into the centre of each
diamond, then carefully spoon over the
glaze. Roast for 20–25 minutes, or until
the fat is brown, glistening and crisp.

8 Grate the rind and squeeze the juice
from the clementines. Simmer all the
cranberry sauce ingredients in a heavy
pan for 15–20 minutes, stirring
frequently. Transfer the sauce to a jug
(pitcher). Serve the ham hot or cold,
garnished with parsley and with the
cranberry sauce.

COOK'S TIPS
• A large stock pot or preserving pan can
be used in place of the casserole or pan
for cooking the ham.
• Leave the ham until it is just cool
enough to handle before removing the
rind. Snip off the string using a sharp
knife or scissors, then carefully slice off
the rind, leaving a thin, even layer of fat.
Use a narrow-bladed, sharp knife for the
best results – a filleting knife, or a long,
slim ham knife would be ideal.

Per portion: Energy 409Kcal/1712kJ; Protein 44g; Carbohydrate 16.8g, of which sugars 16.8g; Fat 18.8g, of which saturates 6.3g; Cholesterol 58mg; Calcium 27mg; Fibre 0.7g; Sodium 2202mg.

PORK CHOPS WITH ONIONS AND MUSTARD

The piquant sauce adds punch and extra flavour to this simple supper dish. Serve it with celeriac and potato mash and a green vegetable, such as broccoli or cabbage.

SERVES FOUR

INGREDIENTS
  4 pork loin chops, at least
    2cm/¾in thick
  30ml/2 tbsp plain (all-purpose)
    flour
  45ml/3 tbsp olive oil
  2 Spanish (Bermuda) onions, sliced
  2 garlic cloves, finely chopped
  250ml/8fl oz/1 cup dry (hard)
    cider
  150ml/¼ pint/⅔ cup chicken stock
  generous pinch of brown sugar
  2 fresh bay leaves
  6 fresh thyme sprigs
  2 strips lemon rind
  120ml/4fl oz/½ cup double
    (heavy) cream
  30–45ml/2–3 tbsp wholegrain
    mustard
  30ml/2 tbsp chopped fresh parsley
  salt and ground black pepper

1 Preheat the oven to 200°C/400°F/Gas 6. Trim the chops of excess fat. Season the flour with salt and pepper and use to coat the chops. Heat 30ml/2 tbsp of the oil in a frying pan and brown the chops on both sides, then transfer them to an ovenproof dish.

2 Add the remaining oil to the pan and cook the onions over a fairly gentle heat until they soften and begin to brown at the edges. Add the garlic and cook for 2 minutes more.

3 Stir in any leftover flour, then gradually stir in the cider and stock. Season well with salt and pepper and add the brown sugar, bay leaves, thyme sprigs and lemon rind. Bring the sauce to the boil, stirring constantly, then pour over the chops.

4 Cover and cook in the oven for 20 minutes. Reduce the heat to 180°C/350°F/Gas 4 and continue cooking for another 30–40 minutes. Remove the foil for the last 10 minutes of the cooking time. Remove the chops from the dish and keep warm, covered with foil.

5 Tip the remaining contents of the dish into a pan or, if the dish is flameproof, place it over a direct heat. Discard the herbs and lemon rind, then bring to the boil.

6 Add the cream and continue to boil, stirring constantly. Taste for seasoning, adding a pinch more sugar if necessary. Finally, stir in the mustard to taste and pour the sauce over the braised chops. Sprinkle with the chopped parsley and serve immediately.

VARIATIONS
• For a less rich sauce, omit the cream and purée the sauce in a blender. Reheat, thinning with a little extra stock if necessary, then adjust the seasoning and add mustard to taste. This will produce a sharper tasting sauce that will need less mustard.
• If you prefer, you can use vegetable or pork stock instead of chicken.
• This recipe also works extremely well with veal chops.

Per portion: Energy 694Kcal/2881kJ; Protein 32g; Carbohydrate 19.8g, of which sugars 9.3g; Fat 53g, of which saturates 21.6g; Cholesterol 131mg; Calcium 80mg; Fibre 2.1g; Sodium 207mg.

ROASTED AND MARINATED PORK

YUAN, A SAUCE MADE FROM SAKE, SHOYU, MIRIN AND CITRUS FRUIT, GIVES A DELICATE FLAVOUR TO THE PORK IN THIS RECIPE. IF POSSIBLE, LEAVE THE MEAT TO MARINATE OVERNIGHT.

SERVES FOUR

INGREDIENTS
   600g/1lb 5oz pork fillet (tenderloin)
   1 garlic clove, crushed
   generous pinch of salt
   4 spring onions (scallions), trimmed, white part only
   10g/¼oz dried wakame, soaked in water for 20 minutes and drained
   10cm/4in celery stick, trimmed and cut in half crossways
   1 carton salad cress
For the yuan sauce
   105ml/7 tbsp shoyu
   45ml/3 tbsp sake
   60ml/4 tbsp mirin
   1 lime, sliced into thin rings

1 Preheat the oven to 200°C/400°F/Gas 6. Rub the pork with crushed garlic and salt, and leave for 15 minutes.

2 Roast the pork for 20 minutes, then turn the meat over and reduce the oven temperature to 180°C/350°F/Gas 4. Cook for a further 20 minutes, or until the pork is cooked. Test by inserting a skewer or the point of a sharp knife into the meat. If the juices run clear, the meat is cooked. If there are any traces of pink in the juices, roast the pork for a little longer.

3 Meanwhile, mix the yuan sauce ingredients in a container that is big enough to hold the pork. When the meat is cooked, immediately put it in the sauce, and leave it to marinate for at least 2 hours, or overnight.

4 Cut the white part of the spring onions in half crossways, then in half lengthways. Remove the round cores, then lay the spring onion quarters flat on a chopping board. Slice them very thinly lengthways to make fine shreds.

5 Soak the shreds in a bowl of ice-cold water. Repeat with the remaining parts of the spring onions. When the shreds curl up, drain and gather them into a loose ball.

6 Cut the drained wakame into 2.5cm/1in squares or narrow strips. Slice the celery very thinly lengthways. Soak in cold water, then drain and gather together as before.

7 Remove the pork from the marinade and wipe with kitchen paper. Slice it very thinly. Strain the marinade and keep it in a gravy boat or jug (pitcher). Arrange the sliced pork on a large serving plate with the vegetables around it. Serve cold with the yuan sauce.

Per portion: Energy 188Kcal/787kJ; Protein 32.5g; Carbohydrate 0.7g, of which sugars 0.6g; Fat 6.1g, of which saturates 2.1g; Cholesterol 95mg; Calcium 18mg; Fibre 0.2g; Sodium 377mg.

POTATO AND SAUSAGE CASSEROLE

YOU WILL FIND NUMEROUS VARIATIONS OF THIS TRADITIONAL SUPPER DISH THROUGHOUT IRELAND, BUT THE BASIC INGREDIENTS ARE THE SAME WHEREVER YOU GO — POTATOES, SAUSAGES AND BACON.

SERVES FOUR

INGREDIENTS
15ml/1 tbsp vegetable oil
4 bacon rashers (strips), cut into
  2.5cm/1in pieces
2 large onions, chopped
2 garlic cloves, crushed
8 large pork sausages
4 large baking potatoes,
  thinly sliced
1.5ml/¼ tsp fresh sage
300ml/½ pint/1¼ cups
  vegetable stock
salt and ground black pepper
freshly baked soda bread,
  to serve (optional)

1 Preheat the oven to 180ºC/350ºF/ Gas 4. Grease a large ovenproof dish and set aside.

2 Heat the oil in a frying pan. Add the bacon and cook for 2 minutes, then add the onions and cook for 5–6 minutes, until golden. Add the garlic and cook for 1 minute, then remove the mixture from the pan and set aside.

3 Add the sausages to the pan and cook for 5–6 minutes, until golden.

4 Arrange the potatoes in the base of the prepared dish. Spoon the bacon and onion mixture on top. Season with the salt and pepper and sprinkle with the fresh sage.

5 Pour on the stock and top with the sausages. Cover and bake for 1 hour. Serve hot with soda bread if you like.

Per portion: Energy 553Kcal/2305kJ; Protein 17.4g; Carbohydrate 48.7g, of which sugars 10g; Fat 33.4g, of which saturates 11.8g; Cholesterol 51mg; Calcium 74mg; Fibre 4g; Sodium 1019mg.

POT-ROASTED BRISKET

THIS JEWISH, POT-ROASTED MEAT DISH INCLUDES THE TRADITIONAL KISHKE, A HEAVY, SAUSAGE-SHAPED DUMPLING, WHICH IS ADDED TO THE POT AND COOKED WITH THE MEAT. SERVE WITH KASHA — MEAT GRAVY WITH KASHA IS ONE OF LIFE'S PERFECT COMBINATIONS.

SERVES SIX TO EIGHT

INGREDIENTS

　5 onions, sliced
　3 bay leaves
　1–1.6kg/2¼–3½lb beef brisket
　1 garlic bulb, broken into cloves
　4 carrots, thickly sliced
　5–10ml/1–2 tsp paprika
　about 500ml/17fl oz/2¼ cups
　　beef stock
　3–4 baking potatoes, peeled
　　and quartered
　salt and ground black pepper
For the kishke
　about 90cm/36in sausage casing
　　(see Cook's Tip)
　250g/9oz/2¼ cups plain
　　(all-purpose) flour
　120ml/4fl oz/½ cup semolina
　　or couscous
　10–15ml/2–3 tsp paprika
　1 carrot, grated and 2 carrots,
　　diced (optional)
　250ml/8fl oz/1 cup rendered
　　chicken fat
　30ml/2 tbsp crisp, fried onions
　½ onion, grated and 3 onions,
　　thinly sliced
　3 garlic cloves, chopped
　salt and ground black pepper

2 Pour in enough stock to fill the dish to about 5–7.5cm/2–3in and cover with foil. Cook in the oven for 2 hours.

3 Meanwhile, make the kishke. In a bowl, combine all the ingredients and stuff the mixture into the casing, leaving enough space for the mixture to expand. Tie into sausage-shaped lengths.

4 When the meat has cooked for about 2 hours, add the kishke and potatoes to the pan, re-cover and cook for a further 1 hour, or until the meat and potatoes are tender.

5 Remove the foil from the dish and increase the oven temperature to 190–200°C/375–400°F/Gas 5–6. Move the onions away from the top of the meat to the side of the dish and return to the oven for a further 30 minutes, or until the meat, onions and potatoes are beginning to brown and become crisp. Serve hot or cold.

COOK'S TIP

Traditionally, sausage casings are used for kishke but, if unavailable, use cooking-strength clear film (plastic wrap) or a piece of muslin (cheesecloth).

1 Preheat the oven to 180°C/350°F/Gas 4. Put one-third of the onions and a bay leaf in an ovenproof dish, then top with the brisket. Sprinkle over the garlic, carrots and the remaining bay leaves, sprinkle with salt, pepper and paprika, then top with the remaining onions.

Per portion: Energy 781Kcal/3271kJ; Protein 44.2g; Carbohydrate 74g, of which sugars 12.7g; Fat 36.4g, of which saturates 14.4g; Cholesterol 113mg; Calcium 124mg; Fibre 5g; Sodium 124mg.

ROAST RIB OF BEEF

THIS ROAST LOOKS SPECTACULAR, AND SERVED IN TRADITIONAL STYLE, WITH YORKSHIRE PUDDINGS AND HORSERADISH SAUCE, IT MAKES A PERFECT CELEBRATION MEAL.

SERVES EIGHT TO TEN

INGREDIENTS
 45ml/3 tbsp mixed peppercorns
 15ml/1 tbsp juniper berries
 2.75kg/6lb rolled rib of beef
 30ml/2 tbsp Dijon mustard
 15ml/1 tbsp olive oil
For the Yorkshire puddings
 150ml/¼ pint/⅔ cup water
 150ml/¼ pint/⅔ cup milk
 115g/4oz/1 cup plain (all-
  purpose) flour
 pinch of salt
 2 eggs, beaten
 60ml/4 tbsp lard, melted, or
  sunflower oil (optional)
For the caramelized shallots
 20 shallots
 5 garlic cloves, peeled
 60ml/4 tbsp light olive oil
 15ml/1 tbsp caster (superfine) sugar
For the gravy
 150ml/¼ pint/⅔ cup red wine
 600ml/1 pint/2½ cups beef stock
 salt and ground black pepper

1 Preheat the oven to 230°C/450°F/ Gas 8. Coarsely crush the peppercorns and juniper berries. Sprinkle half the spices over the meat, then transfer to a roasting pan and roast for 30 minutes.

COOK'S TIP
If you prefer to cook beef on the bone, buy a 3.6kg/8lb forerib. Trim off the excess fat, sprinkle over the spices, then follow the instructions in steps 1 and 2. Roast at the lower temperature for 2 hours for rare beef, 2½ hours for medium rare, and 3 hours for well done.

2 Reduce the oven temperature to 180°C/350°F/Gas 4. Mix the mustard and oil into the remaining crushed spices and spread the resulting paste over the meat. Roast the meat for a further 1¼ hours if you like your meat rare, 1 hour 50 minutes for a medium-rare result or 2 hours 25 minutes for a roast that is medium to well done. Baste the beef frequently during cooking.

3 Make the Yorkshire puddings as soon as the beef is in the oven. Stir the water into the milk. Sift the flour and salt into a bowl. Make a well in the middle and gradually whisk in the eggs followed by the milk and water to make a smooth batter. Cover and leave to stand for about 1 hour. (The batter can be made well in advance and chilled overnight in the refrigerator if convenient.)

4 An hour before the beef is due to be ready, mix the shallots and garlic cloves with the light olive oil and spoon into the roasting pan around the beef. After 30 minutes, sprinkle the caster sugar over the shallots and garlic. Stir the shallots and garlic two or three times during cooking.

5 Transfer the meat to a large serving platter, cover tightly with foil and set aside in a warm place for 20–30 minutes. (This resting time makes carving easier.) Increase the oven temperature to 230°C/450°F/ Gas 8. Divide 60ml/4 tbsp dripping from the meat or the lard or oil, if using, among 10 individual Yorkshire pudding tins (muffin pans) and heat in the oven for 5 minutes.

6 Spoon the Yorkshire pudding batter into the hot fat in the tins and bake for 20–30 minutes, or until risen, firm and a golden brown colour. The time depends on the size of the tins: larger Yorkshire puddings will take longer than those in smaller tins.

7 Make the gravy while the Yorkshire puddings are cooking. Simmer the red wine and beef stock together in a pan for about 5 minutes to intensify the flavour of the gravy.

8 Skim the fat from the meat juices in the roasting pan, then pour in the wine mixture and simmer until the gravy is reduced and thickened slightly to a syrupy consistency. Stir frequently with a wooden spoon to remove all of the roasting residue from the roasting pan. Season to taste.

9 Serve the beef with the individual Yorkshire puddings, caramelized shallots and gravy. Offer roast potatoes or game chips as accompaniments, along with a selection of lightly cooked, seasonal vegetables.

Per portion: Energy 828Kcal/3444kJ; Protein 64.8g; Carbohydrate 14.2g, of which sugars 3.3g; Fat 55.7g, of which saturates 22.9g; Cholesterol 229mg; Calcium 74mg; Fibre 0.7g; Sodium 137mg.

ROAST LEG OF LAMB

When young lamb was seasonal to springtime, a roast leg was an Easter speciality, served with a sauce using the first sprigs of mint of the year and early new potatoes. Roast lamb is now well established as a year-round family favourite for Sunday lunch, often served with crisp roast potatoes.

SERVES SIX

INGREDIENTS

    1.5kg/3¼lb leg of lamb
    4 garlic cloves, sliced
    2 fresh rosemary sprigs
    30ml/2 tbsp light olive oil
    300ml/½ pint/1¼ cups red wine
    5ml/1 tsp clear honey
    45ml/3 tbsp redcurrant jelly
    salt and ground black pepper
For the roast potatoes
    45ml/3 tbsp white vegetable fat
      or lard
    1.3kg/3lb potatoes, such as Desirée,
      cut into chunks
For the mint sauce
    about 15g/½oz fresh mint
    10ml/2 tsp caster (superfine) sugar
    15ml/1 tbsp boiling water
    30ml/2 tbsp white wine vinegar

1 Preheat the oven to 220°C/425°F/ Gas 7. Make small slits into the lamb all over the leg. Press a slice of garlic and a few rosemary leaves into each slit, then place the lamb in a roasting pan and season well. Drizzle the oil over the lamb and roast for about 1 hour.

COOK'S TIP

To make a quick and tasty gravy from the pan juices, add about 300ml/½ pint/ 1¼ cups red wine, stock or water and boil, stirring occasionally, until reduced and well-flavoured. Season to taste, then strain into a sauce boat to serve.

2 Meanwhile, mix the wine, honey and redcurrant jelly in a small pan and heat, stirring, until the jelly melts. Bring to the boil, then reduce the heat and simmer until reduced by half. Spoon this glaze over the lamb and return it to the oven for 30–45 minutes.

3 To make the potatoes, put the fat in a roasting pan on the oven shelf above the meat. Boil the potatoes for about 5–10 minutes, then drain them and fluff up the surface of each with a fork.

4 Add the prepared potatoes to the hot fat and baste well, then roast them for 40–50 minutes, or until they are crisp.

5 Meanwhile, make the mint sauce. Place the mint on a chopping board and sprinkle the sugar over the top. Chop the mint finely, then transfer the mint and sugar to a bowl.

6 Add the boiling water and stir until the sugar has dissolved. Add 15ml/ 1 tbsp vinegar and taste the sauce before adding the remaining vinegar. (You may want to add slightly less or more than the suggested quantity.) Leave the mint sauce to stand until you are ready to serve the meal.

7 Cover the lamb with foil and set it aside in a warm place to rest for 10–15 minutes before carving. Serve with the crisp roast potatoes, mint sauce and a selection of seasonal vegetables.

Per portion: Energy 732Kcal/3080kJ; Protein 78g; Carbohydrate 36.4g, of which sugars 4.2g; Fat 31.6g, of which saturates 12.7g; Cholesterol 257mg; Calcium 36mg; Fibre 2.2g; Sodium 182mg.

PIZZAS, PASTRIES
& PIES

Home-made pizzas are more delicious than take-away ones

and are fun to make. Making your own allows you to mix and

match toppings as much as you want. Here, you'll find tasty

ideas such as Sun-dried Tomato Calzone, Hot Pepperoni Pizza

and Pissaladiere. This chapter also includes delectable pastries

like Salmon in Puff Pastry, and you will also find many

family favourites, such as Steak, Mushroom and Ale Pie —

an ideal dish to serve when entertaining as you can prepare it

in advance and leave to cook in the oven.

SUN-DRIED TOMATO CALZONE

CALZONE IS A TRADITIONAL FOLDED PIZZA. IN THIS TASTY VEGETARIAN VERSION, YOU CAN ADD MORE OR LESS RED CHILLI FLAKES, DEPENDING ON PERSONAL TASTE.

SERVES TWO

INGREDIENTS
    4 baby aubergines (eggplant)
    3 shallots, chopped
    45ml/3 tbsp olive oil
    1 garlic clove, chopped
    50g/2oz/⅓ cup sun-dried tomatoes
       in oil, drained
    1.5ml/¼ tsp dried red chilli flakes,
       if using
    10ml/2 tsp chopped fresh thyme
    75g/3oz mozzarella cheese, cubed
    salt and ground black pepper
    15–30ml/1–2 tbsp freshly grated
       Parmesan cheese, plus extra
       to serve
For the dough
    225g/8oz/2 cups strong white
       bread flour
    5ml/1 tsp salt
    2.5ml/½ tsp easy-blend (rapid-rise)
       dried yeast
    15ml/1 tbsp olive oil
    150ml/¼ pint/⅔ cup warm water

1 Make the dough. Place the dry ingredients in a bowl and mix to form a soft dough with the oil and water. Knead for 10 minutes. Put in an oiled bowl, cover and leave in a warm place until doubled in size.

2 Preheat the oven to 220°C/425°F/ Gas 7. Dice the aubergines. Cook the shallots in a little oil until soft. Add the aubergines, garlic, sun-dried tomatoes, chilli, if using, thyme and seasoning. Cook for 5 minutes.

3 Divide the dough in half and roll out each piece on a lightly floured work surface to an 18cm/7in round.

4 Spread the aubergine mixture over half of each round, leaving a 2.5cm/1in border, then sprinkle on the mozzarella. Dampen the edges with water, then fold over the dough to enclose the filling. Press the edges firmly together to seal. Place on greased baking sheets.

5 Brush with half the remaining oil and make a small hole in the top of each calzone to allow steam to escape. Bake for 15–20 minutes, until golden.

6 Remove from the oven and brush with the remaining oil. Sprinkle over the Parmesan and serve immediately.

Per portion: Energy 777Kcal/3259kJ; Protein 25.3g; Carbohydrate 92.2g, of which sugars 6.2g; Fat 36.7g, of which saturates 11.8g; Cholesterol 37mg; Calcium 494mg; Fibre 7g; Sodium 323mg.

PEPPERY TOMATO PIZZA

PUNGENT ROCKET AND AROMATIC FRESH BASIL ADD COLOUR AND FLAVOUR TO THIS CRISP PIZZA,
A PERFECT ADDITION TO ANY PICNIC, BUFFET OR OUTDOOR MEAL.

SERVES TWO

INGREDIENTS
    10ml/2 tsp olive oil
    1 garlic clove, crushed
    150g/5oz can chopped tomatoes
    2.5ml/½ tsp caster (superfine) sugar
    30ml/2 tbsp torn fresh basil leaves
    2 tomatoes, seeded and chopped
    150g/5oz mozzarella cheese, sliced
    20g/¾oz rocket (arugula) leaves
For the pizza base
    225g/8oz/2 cups strong white
        bread flour
    5ml/1 tsp salt
    2.5ml/½ tsp easy-blend (rapid-rise)
        dried yeast
    30ml/2 tbsp olive oil

1 To make the pizza base, place the dry ingredients in a bowl. Add the oil and 150ml/¼ pint/⅔ cup warm water. Mix to form a soft dough.

2 Turn out the dough and knead until it is smooth and elastic. Place in an oiled bowl and cover. Leave in a warm place for 45 minutes, or until doubled in bulk.

3 Preheat the oven to 220°C/425°F/ Gas 7. Make the topping. Heat the oil in a frying pan and cook the garlic for 1 minute. Add the canned tomatoes and sugar and cook for 10 minutes.

4 Knead the risen dough lightly, then roll out to form a rough 30cm/12in round. Place on a lightly oiled baking sheet and push up the edges of the dough to form a shallow, even rim.

5 Season the tomato mixture and stir in the basil. Spoon it over the pizza base, then top with the chopped fresh tomatoes. Arrange the mozzarella slices on top of the tomato mixture. Season with sea salt and pepper and drizzle with a little olive oil.

6 Bake for 10–12 minutes, until crisp and golden. Scatter the rocket leaves over the pizza just before serving.

Per portion: Energy 735Kcal/3087kJ; Protein 26.1g; Carbohydrate 93g, of which sugars 7.3g; Fat 31.3g, of which saturates 12.7g; Cholesterol 44mg; Calcium 459mg; Fibre 5.5g; Sodium 330mg.

BRESAOLA AND ROCKET PIZZA

ALTHOUGH THE ARMENIANS ORIGINATED THE IDEA OF TOPPING FLATTENED DOUGH WITH SAVOURY INGREDIENTS BEFORE BAKING IT, IT WAS THE ITALIANS — THE NEAPOLITANS IN PARTICULAR — WHO DEVELOPED THE PIZZA IN THE 1830s.

SERVES FOUR

INGREDIENTS
    150g/5oz packet pizza base mix
    120ml/4fl oz/½ cup lukewarm water
    225g/8oz/3¼ cups mixed
     wild mushrooms
    25g/1oz/2 tbsp butter
    2 garlic cloves, coarsely chopped
    60ml/4 tbsp pesto
    8 slices bresaola
    4 tomatoes, sliced
    75g/3oz/⅓ cup cream cheese
    25g/1oz rocket (arugula)

1 Preheat the oven to 200°C/400°F/ Gas 6. Tip the packet of pizza base mix into a large mixing bowl and pour in enough of the water to mix to a soft, not sticky, dough, following the instructions on the packet.

2 Turn out the dough on to a lightly floured surface and knead for about 5 minutes, or until smooth and elastic. Divide the dough into two equal pieces, knead lightly to form two balls, then pat out the balls of dough into flat rounds with your hands.

3 Roll out each piece of dough on a lightly floured surface to a 23cm/9in round and transfer to baking sheets.

4 Slice the wild mushrooms. Melt the butter in a frying pan and cook the garlic for 2 minutes. Add the mushrooms and cook over a high heat for about 5 minutes, or until the mushrooms have softened but are not overcooked.

5 Spread pesto on the pizza bases, to within 2cm/¾in of the edge of each one. Arrange the bresaola and tomato slices around the rims of the pizzas, then spoon the cooked mushrooms into the middle.

6 Dot the cream cheese on top of the pizzas and bake for 15–18 minutes, or until the bases are crisp and the cheese just melted. Top each pizza with a handful of rocket leaves just before serving. Serve immediately.

COOK'S TIP
If you are in a hurry, buy two ready-made pizza bases instead of the pizza mix and bake for 10 minutes.

Per portion: Energy 448Kcal/1873kJ; Protein 16.6g; Carbohydrate 34.7g, of which sugars 6g; Fat 28g, of which saturates 12.8g; Cholesterol 56mg; Calcium 179mg; Fibre 3.5g; Sodium 213mg.

HOT PEPPERONI PIZZA

THERE IS NOTHING MORE MOUTHWATERING THAN A FRESHLY BAKED PIZZA, ESPECIALLY WHEN THE TOPPING INCLUDES TOMATOES, MOZZARELLA CHEESE, PEPPERONI AND RED CHILLIES.

SERVES FOUR

INGREDIENTS
   225g/8oz/2 cups strong white
    bread flour
   10ml/2 tsp easy-blend (rapid-rise)
    dried yeast
   5ml/1 tsp granulated sugar
   2.5ml/½ tsp salt
   15ml/1 tbsp olive oil
   175ml/6fl oz/¾ cup mixed lukewarm
    milk and water
For the topping
   400g/14oz can chopped
    tomatoes, strained
   2 garlic cloves, crushed
   5ml/1 tsp dried oregano
   225g/8oz mozzarella cheese, grated
   2 dried red chillies, crumbled
   225g/8oz pepperoni, sliced
   30ml/2 tbsp drained capers
   fresh oregano, to garnish

1 Sift the flour, stir in the yeast, sugar and salt and make a well in the centre. Stir the oil into the milk and water, then stir into the flour. Mix to a soft dough.

2 Knead the dough on a lightly floured surface for 10 minutes until it is smooth and elastic. Cover and leave in a warm place for about 30 minutes, or until the dough has doubled in bulk.

3 Preheat the oven to 220°C/425°F/ Gas 7. Turn the dough out on to a lightly floured surface and knead lightly for 1 minute. Divide it in half and roll each piece out to a 25cm/10in round. Place on lightly oiled pizza trays or baking sheets. To make the topping, mix the strained tomatoes, garlic and dried oregano in a bowl.

4 Spread half the tomato mixture over each base, leaving a border around the edge. Set half the mozzarella aside. Divide the rest between the pizzas, sprinkling it over evenly. Bake for 7–10 minutes, until the dough rim on each pizza is pale golden.

5 Sprinkle the crumbled chillies over the pizzas, then arrange the pepperoni slices and capers on top. Sprinkle with the remaining mozzarella. Return the pizzas to the oven and bake for 7–10 minutes more. Sprinkle over the fresh oregano and serve immediately.

Per portion: Energy 631Kcal/2638kJ; Protein 28.8g; Carbohydrate 47.6g, of which sugars 4.7g; Fat 37.5g, of which saturates 16.8g; Cholesterol 80mg; Calcium 317mg; Fibre 2.7g; Sodium 1498mg.

PISSALADIÈRE

This famous onion and anchovy dish is a traditional market food of Nice in southern France. It can be made using either shortcrust pastry or, as here, yeasted dough, similar to a pizza base. Either way, it is most delicious eaten lukewarm rather than piping hot.

SERVES SIX

INGREDIENTS
 250g/9oz/2¼ cups strong white bread
  flour, plus extra for dusting
 50g/2oz/⅓ cup fine polenta
  or semolina
 5ml/1 tsp salt
 175ml/6fl oz/¾ cup lukewarm water
 5ml/1 tsp dried yeast
 5ml/1 tsp caster (superfine) sugar
 30ml/2 tbsp extra virgin olive oil
For the topping
 60–75ml/4–5 tbsp extra virgin
  olive oil
 6 large sweet Spanish (Bermuda)
  onions, thinly sliced
 2 large garlic cloves, thinly sliced
 5ml/1 tsp chopped fresh thyme, plus
  several sprigs
 1 fresh rosemary sprig
 1–2 x 50g/2oz cans anchovies in
  olive oil
 50–75g/2–3oz small black olives,
  preferably small Niçoise olives
 salt and ground black pepper

1 Mix the flour, polenta or semolina and salt in a large mixing bowl. Pour half the water into a bowl. Add the yeast and sugar, then leave in a warm place for 10 minutes, until frothy. Pour the yeast mixture into the flour mixture with the remaining water and the olive oil.

2 Using your hands, mix all the ingredients together to form a dough, then turn out and knead for 5 minutes, until smooth, springy and elastic.

3 Return the dough to the clean, floured bowl and place it in a plastic bag or cover with oiled clear film (plastic wrap), then set the dough aside at room temperature for 30–60 minutes to rise and double in bulk.

4 Meanwhile, start to prepare the topping. Heat 45ml/3 tbsp of the olive oil in a large, heavy pan and add the sliced onions. Stir well to coat the onions in the oil, then cover the pan and cook over a very low heat, stirring occasionally, for 20-30 minutes. (Use a heat-diffuser mat to keep the heat low, if possible.)

5 Add a little salt to taste and the garlic, chopped thyme and rosemary sprig. Stir well and continue cooking for another 15–25 minutes, or until the onions are soft and deep golden yellow but not browned at all. Uncover the pan for the last 5–10 minutes' cooking if the onions seem very wet. Remove and discard the rosemary. Set the onions aside to cool.

6 Preheat the oven to 220°C/425°F/ Gas 7. Roll out the dough thinly and use to line a large baking sheet, about 30 x 23–25cm/12 x 9–10in. Taste the onions for seasoning before spreading them over the dough.

7 Drain the anchovies, cut them in half lengthways and arrange them in a lattice pattern over the onions. Sprinkle the olives and thyme sprigs over the top of the pissaladière and drizzle with the remaining olive oil. Bake for about 20–25 minutes, or until the dough is browned and cooked. Season with pepper and serve warm, cut into slices.

VARIATIONS
• Shortcrust pastry can be used instead of yeast dough as a base: bake it blind for 10–15 minutes before adding the filling.
• If you enjoy anchovies, try spreading about 60ml/4 tbsp anchovy purée (paste) – *anchoïade* – over the base before adding the onions. Alternatively, spread black olive paste over the base.

Per portion: Energy 431Kcal/1797kJ; Protein 9.9g; Carbohydrate 51.6g, of which sugars 10g; Fat 21.7g, of which saturates 3.1g; Cholesterol 8mg; Calcium 138mg; Fibre 3.8g; Sodium 825mg.

SALMON IN PUFF PASTRY

THIS IS AN ELEGANT PARTY DISH, MADE WITH RICE, EGGS AND SALMON ENCLOSED IN PUFF PASTRY.

SERVES SIX

INGREDIENTS

    450g/1lb puff pastry, thawed
      if frozen
    1 egg, beaten
    3 hard-boiled eggs
    90ml/6 tbsp single (light) cream
    200g/7oz/1¾ cups cooked long
      grain rice
    30ml/2 tbsp finely chopped
      fresh parsley
    10ml/2 tsp chopped fresh tarragon
    675g/1½lb salmon fillets
    40g/1½oz/3 tbsp butter
    juice of ½ lemon
    salt and ground black pepper

2 In a bowl, mash the hard-boiled eggs with the cream, then stir in the cooked rice. Add the parsley and tarragon and season well. Spoon this mixture on to the prepared pastry.

5 Roll out the remaining pastry and cut out a semi-circular piece to cover the head portion and a tail shape to cover the tail. Brush both pieces of pastry with a little beaten egg and place on top of the fish, pressing down firmly to secure. Score a criss-cross pattern on the tail.

1 Preheat the oven to 190°C/375°F/ Gas 5. Roll out two-thirds of the pastry into a large oval, measuring about 35cm/14in in length. Cut into a curved fish shape and place on a lightly greased baking sheet. Use the trimmings to make narrow strips. Brush one side of each strip with a little beaten egg and secure in place around the rim of the pastry to make a raised edge. Prick the base all over with a fork, then bake for 8–10 minutes until the sides are well risen and the pastry is lightly golden. Leave to cool.

3 Cut the salmon into 2cm/¾in chunks. Melt the butter until it starts to sizzle, then add the salmon. Turn the pieces over in the butter so that they begin to colour but do not cook through.

4 Remove from the heat and arrange the salmon pieces on top of the rice, piled in the centre. Stir the lemon juice into the butter in the pan, then spoon the mixture over the salmon pieces.

6 Cut the remaining pastry into small rounds and, starting from the tail end, arrange the rounds in overlapping lines to represent scales. Add an extra one for an eye. Brush the whole fish shape with the remaining beaten egg.

7 Bake for 10 minutes, then reduce the temperature to 160°C/325°F/Gas 3 and cook for a further 15–20 minutes, until the pastry is evenly golden. Slide the fish on to a serving plate and serve.

COOK'S TIP

If the pastry seems to be browning too quickly, cover it with foil during cooking and remove from the oven for the last 5 minutes. It is important that the "fish" cooks for the recommended time, so that the salmon is sufficiently cooked through.

VARIATION

If time is short you may prefer to use this simplified method. Roll out the pastry into a rectangle, then make pastry edges to contain the filling. Part bake the pastry, add the filling, top with plain, rolled out pastry and return it to the oven.

Per portion: Energy 668Kcal/2782kJ; Protein 31g; Carbohydrate 36.6g, of which sugars 0.7g; Fat 45.3g, of which saturates 14g; Cholesterol 209mg; Calcium 98mg; Fibre 1.1g; Sodium 389mg.

COD, BASIL, TOMATO AND POTATO PIE

FRESH AND SMOKED FISH MAKE A GREAT COMBINATION, ESPECIALLY WITH THE HINT OF TOMATO AND BASIL. SERVED WITH A GREEN SALAD, THIS MAKES AN IDEAL DISH FOR LUNCH OR A FAMILY SUPPER.

2 Melt 75g/3oz/6 tbsp of the butter in a large pan, add the onion and cook for about 5 minutes, until softened and tender but not browned. Sprinkle over the flour and half the chopped basil. Gradually add the reserved fish cooking liquid, adding a little more milk if necessary to make a fairly thin sauce, stirring constantly to make a smooth consistency. Bring to the boil, season with salt and pepper, and add the remaining basil.

3 Remove the pan from the heat, then add the fish and tomatoes and stir gently to combine. Pour into an ovenproof dish.

SERVES EIGHT

INGREDIENTS
  1kg/2¼lb smoked cod fillets
  1kg/2¼lb fresh cod fillets
  900ml/1½ pint/3¾ cups milk
  1.2litres/2 pints/5 cups water
  2 fresh basil sprigs
  1 fresh lemon thyme sprig
  150g/5oz/⅔ cup butter
  1 onion, chopped
  75g/3oz/⅔ cup plain
   (all-purpose) flour
  30ml/2 tbsp chopped fresh basil
  4 firm plum tomatoes, peeled
   and chopped
  12 medium floury potatoes
  salt and ground black pepper
  crushed black pepper corns,
   to garnish
  lettuce leaves, to serve

1 Place both kinds of fish in a roasting pan with 600ml/1 pint/2½ cups of the milk, the water and the herb sprigs. Bring to a simmer and cook gently for about 3–4 minutes. Remove from the heat and leave the fish to cool in the liquid for about 20 minutes. Drain the fish, reserving the cooking liquid for use in the sauce. Flake the fish, removing the skin and any remaining bones.

4 Preheat the oven to 180°C/350°F/ Gas 4. Cook the potatoes in boiling water until tender. Drain then add the remaining butter and milk and mash. Season to taste and spoon over the fish mixture, using a fork to create a pattern. You can freeze the pie at this stage. Bake for 30 minutes until the top is golden. Sprinkle with the crushed pepper corns and serve hot with lettuce.

Per portion: Energy 474Kcal/1989kJ; Protein 49.6g; Carbohydrate 30.7g, of which sugars 4.6g; Fat 17.8g, of which saturates 10.2g; Cholesterol 155mg; Calcium 62mg; Fibre 2.5g; Sodium 1672mg.

TAMALE PIE

THIS IS A TEXAN VERSION OF A TRADITIONAL MEXICAN RECIPE, ALTHOUGH SO MANY VARIATIONS EXIST THAT BOTH SIDES OF THE BORDER CAN CLAIM THE ORIGINAL.

SERVES EIGHT

INGREDIENTS

   115g/4oz bacon, chopped
   1 onion, finely chopped
   450g/1lb lean minced (ground) beef
   10–15ml/2–3 tsp chilli powder
   5ml/1 tsp salt
   400g/14oz can tomatoes
   40g/1½oz/⅓ cup chopped
     black olives
   175g/6oz/1 cup corn kernels, freshly
     cooked or thawed frozen
   120ml/4fl oz/½ cup sour cream
   115g/4oz/1 cup grated Cheddar or
     Monterey Jack cheese
For the tamale topping
   250–300ml/8–10fl oz/1–1¼ cups
     chicken stock
   175g/6oz/1½ cups masa harina
     or cornmeal
   90ml/6 tbsp margarine or
     vegetable shortening
   2.5ml/½ tsp baking powder
   50ml/2fl oz/¼ cup milk
   salt and ground black pepper

1 Preheat the oven to 190°C/375°F/ Gas 5. Cook the bacon in a large, heavy frying pan for 2–3 minutes, until the fat runs. Pour off any excess fat, leaving 15–30ml/1–2 tbsp. Add the onion and cook, over a medium heat, stirring occasionally, for about 5 minutes, until just softened.

2 Add the beef, chilli powder and salt and cook for 5 minutes, stirring to break up the meat. Stir in the tomatoes and cook for 5 minutes more, breaking them up with a spoon.

3 Add the olives, corn, and sour cream, and mix well. Transfer to a 38cm/15in long rectangular or oval ovenproof dish. Set aside.

4 To make the topping, bring the chicken stock to the boil in a pan over a medium heat and season it with salt and pepper if necessary.

5 In a food processor, combine the masa harina or cornmeal, margarine or shortening, baking powder and milk. Process until combined. With the machine still running, gradually pour in the hot stock until a smooth, thick batter is formed. If the batter is too thick to spread, add additional hot stock or water, a little at a time.

6 Pour the batter over the top of the beef mixture, spreading it evenly with a metal spatula.

7 Bake for about 20 minutes, until the top is just browned. Sprinkle the surface evenly with the grated cheese and continue baking for a further 10–15 minutes, until the cheese has melted. Serve immediately.

Per portion: Energy 492Kcal/2044kJ; Protein 23.3g; Carbohydrate 26.6g, of which sugars 6.1g; Fat 32.1g, of which saturates 17.4g; Cholesterol 96mg; Calcium 206mg; Fibre 1.6g; Sodium 827mg.

CHICKEN-MUSHROOM PIE

THIS IS A GREAT FAMILY FAVOURITE, ESPECIALLY POPULAR ON A COLD WINTER'S EVENING. IT'S ALSO A GOOD WAY TO USE UP LEFTOVER ROAST CHICKEN.

SERVES SIX

INGREDIENTS
- 15g/½oz dried porcini mushrooms
- 50g/2oz/¼ cup butter
- 30ml/2 tbsp flour
- 250ml/8fl oz/1 cup simmering chicken stock
- 50ml/2fl oz/¼ cup whipping cream or milk
- 1 onion, coarsely chopped
- 2 carrots, sliced
- 2 celery sticks, coarsely chopped
- 50g/2oz fresh mushrooms, quartered
- 450g/1lb cooked chicken meat, cubed
- 50g/2oz/½ cup shelled fresh or frozen peas
- beaten egg, for glazing
- salt and ground black pepper

For the pastry
- 225g/8oz/2 cups plain (all-purpose) flour
- 1.5ml/¼ tsp salt
- 115g/4oz/½ cup cold butter, cut into pieces
- 75g/3oz/⅓ cup shortening
- 60–120ml/4–8 tbsp iced water

1 For the pastry, sift the flour and salt into a bowl. With a pastry blender or two knives, cut in the butter and shortening until the mixture resembles coarse breadcrumbs. Sprinkle with 90ml/6 tbsp iced water and mix until the dough holds together. If the dough is too crumbly, add a little more water, 15ml/1 tbsp at a time. Gather the dough into a ball and flatten into a round. Wrap in greaseproof (waxed) paper and chill for at least 30 minutes.

2 Place the dried porcini mushrooms in a small bowl. Add hot water to cover and leave to soak for about 30 minutes until softened. Lift out of the water with a slotted spoon, leaving any grit behind, and drain. Discard the soaking water.

3 Preheat the oven to 190°C/375°F/Gas 5. Melt 30ml/2 tbsp of the butter in a heavy pan. Stir in the flour and cook, whisking constantly, for about 1 minute, until bubbling. Gradually, add the warm stock and cook over a medium heat, whisking constantly, until the mixture comes to the boil. Cook, still whisking, for 2–3 minutes more. Whisk in the cream or milk and season to taste with salt and pepper. Remove the pan from the heat and set aside.

4 Heat the remaining butter in a large, non-stick frying pan until foaming. Add the onion and carrots and cook over a medium heat, stirring occasionally, for about 5 minutes, until softened. Add the celery and fresh mushrooms and cook, stirring occasionally, for a further 5 minutes. Stir in the cubed chicken meat, fresh or frozen peas, and drained porcini mushrooms.

5 Add the chicken mixture to the cream sauce and stir to mix. Taste for seasoning. Transfer to a 2 litre/4 pint/10 cup rectangular ovenproof dish.

6 Roll out the dough on a lightly floured surface to about 3mm/⅛in thickness. Cut out a rectangle about 2.5cm/1in larger all around than the dish. Lay the rectangle of dough over the filling. Make a decorative edge, crimping the dough by pushing the index finger of one hand between the thumb and index finger of the other hand.

7 Cut several vents in the top of the pie to allow steam to escape. Brush the dough with the egg glaze.

8 Press together the dough trimmings, then roll out again. Cut into strips and lay them over the top of the pie. Glaze again. If you like, roll small balls of dough and set them in the "windows" in the lattice.

9 Bake for about 30 minutes, until the top of the pie is browned and the filling is piping hot. Serve the pie hot, straight from the dish.

Per portion: Energy 600Kcal/2501kJ; Protein 23.7g; Carbohydrate 38.8g, of which sugars 3.7g; Fat 40g, of which saturates 21.8g; Cholesterol 132mg; Calcium 92mg; Fibre 2.7g; Sodium 226mg.

STEAK, MUSHROOM AND ALE PIE

THIS ANGLO-IRISH DISH IS A FIRM FAVOURITE ON MENUS AT RESTAURANTS SPECIALIZING IN TRADITIONAL FARE. PIPING HOT, CREAMY MASHED POTATOES OR PARSLEY-DRESSED BOILED POTATOES AND SLIGHTLY CRUNCHY CARROTS AND GREEN BEANS OR CABBAGE ARE PERFECT ACCOMPANIMENTS; FOR A BAR-STYLE MEAL, CHIPS OR BAKED POTATOES AND A SIDE SALAD CAN BE SERVED WITH THE PIE.

SERVES FOUR

INGREDIENTS

25g/1oz/2 tbsp butter
1 large onion, finely chopped
115g/4oz/1½ cups chestnut or button
  (white) mushrooms, halved
900g/2lb lean beef in one piece,
  such as braising steak
30ml/2 tbsp plain (all-purpose) flour
45ml/3 tbsp sunflower oil
300ml/½ pint/1¼ cups stout or
  brown ale
300ml/½ pint/1¼ cups beef stock
  or consommé
500g/1¼lb puff pastry, thawed if frozen
beaten egg, to glaze
salt and ground black pepper

1 Melt the butter in a large, flameproof casserole, add the onion and cook gently, stirring occasionally, for about 5 minutes, or until it is softened but not coloured. Add the halved mushrooms and continue cooking for a further 5 minutes, stirring occasionally.

2 Meanwhile, trim the meat and cut it into 2.5cm/1in cubes. Season the flour and toss the meat in it.

COOK'S TIP
To make individual pies, divide the filling among four individual pie dishes. Cut the pastry into quarters and cover as above. If the dishes do not have rims, press a narrow strip of pastry around the edge of each dish to seal the lid in place. Cook as above, reducing the cooking time slightly.

3 Use a slotted spoon to remove the onion mixture from the casserole and set aside. Add and heat the oil, then brown the steak, in batches, over a high heat to seal in the juices.

4 Replace the vegetables, then stir in the stout or ale and stock or consommé. Bring to the boil, reduce the heat and simmer for about 1 hour, stirring occasionally, or until the meat is tender. Season to taste and transfer to a 1.5 litre/2½ pint/6¼ cup pie dish. Cover and leave to cool. If possible, chill the meat filling overnight as this allows the flavour to develop. Preheat the oven to 230°C/450°F/Gas 8.

5 Roll out the pastry in the shape of the dish and about 4cm/1½in larger all around. Cut a 2.5cm/1in strip from the edge of the pastry. Brush the rim of the dish with water and press the pastry strip on it. Brush the pastry rim with beaten egg and cover the pie with the pastry lid. Press the lid firmly in place and then trim the excess from around the edge.

6 Use the blunt edge of a knife to tap the outside edge of the pastry, pressing it down with your finger as you seal in the filling. (This technique is known as knocking up.)

7 Pinch the pastry between your fingers to flute the edge. Roll out any remaining pastry trimmings and cut out shapes to garnish the pie, brushing the shapes with a little beaten egg before pressing them lightly in place.

8 Make a hole in the middle of the pie to allow steam to escape, brush the top carefully with beaten egg and chill for 10 minutes to rest the pastry.

9 Bake the pie for 15 minutes, then reduce the oven temperature to 200°C/400°F/Gas 6 and bake for a further 15–20 minutes, or until the pastry is risen and golden.

Per portion: Energy 1061Kcal/4423kJ; Protein 58.8g; Carbohydrate 59.3g, of which sugars 7.6g; Fat 65.3g, of which saturates 24g; Cholesterol 164mg; Calcium 129mg; Fibre 3.2g; Sodium 622mg.

INDEX